PENGUIN BOOKS

INC. YOUR DREAMS

Rebecca Maddox is the President of Capital Rose, Inc., a company that provides women business owners access to financing, information, and related products, and works with Fortune 500 clients to capitalize on the growing opportunities in the women's market. Ms. Maddox has held senior executive positions at Capital Holding, Citicorp, and Comp-U-Card of America. She has an MBA from Columbia University and is a Certified Public Accountant in New York State. She lives on a horse farm in Chester Springs, Pennsylvania.

PENGUIN BOOKS

PENGUIN BOOKS
Published by the Penguin Group
Penguin Books USA Inc., 375 Hudson Street, New York, New York 10014, U.S.A.
Penguin Books Ltd, 27 Wrights Lane, London W8 5TZ, England
Penguin Books Australia Ltd, Ringwood, Victoria, Australia
Penguin Books Canada Ltd, 10 Alcorn Avenue, Toronto, Ontario, Canada M4V 3B2
Penguin Books (N.Z.) Ltd, 182–190 Wairau Road, Auckland 10, New Zealand

Penguin Books Ltd, Registered Offices: Harmondsworth, Middlesex, England

First published in the United States of America by Viking Penguin,
a division of Penguin Books USA Inc., 1995
Published in Penguin Books 1996

1 3 5 7 9 10 8 6 4 2

Grateful acknowledgment is made for permission to use selections from
the following copyrighted works:
Speech by John W. Gardner. By permission of John W. Gardner.
Golf My Way by Jack Nicklaus and Ken Bowden, Simon & Schuster.
Reprinted by permission of the authors.
"The Dream Ride: A Path to Yourself," a guided-imagery audiotape by Marilyn O. Sifford.
By permission of Marilyn O. Sifford.
"Letters to Alicia" by John Steinbeck, appearing in *Newsday*, April 23, 1966.
Copyright © 1966 by John Steinbeck. Copyright © renewed 1994 by Elaine Steinbeck and
Thom Steinbeck. Reprinted by permission of McIntosh and Otis, Inc.

THE LIBRARY OF CONGRESS HAS CATALOGUED THE HARDCOVER AS FOLLOWS:
Maddox, Rebecca J.
Inc. your dreams/Rebecca J. Maddox.
p. cm.
ISBN 0-670-85433-6 (hc.)
ISBN 0 14 02.3537 X (pbk.)
1. Self-employed women. 2. Women-owned business enterprises. I. Title.
HD6072.5.M33 1995
658′.041′082—dc20 95-1448

Printed in the United States of America
Set in Bembo

To my Grandmother

Marie Zeller

For believing in me

Meaning is not something you stumble across, like the answer to a riddle or the prize in a treasure hunt. Meaning is something you build into your life. You build it out of your own past, out of your affections and loyalties, out of the experience of humankind as it is passed on to you, out of your own talent and understanding, out of the things you believe in, out of the things and people you love, out of the values for which you are willing to sacrifice something. The ingredients are there. You are the only one who can put them together into that unique pattern that will be your life. Let it be a life that has dignity and meaning for you. If it does, then the particular balance of success or failure is of less account.

—*John W. Gardner*

Author of Excellence *and* Self-Renewal

CONTENTS

PREFACE

ON THE SURFACE OF IT, this book is about deciding whether or not you should become a business owner. On a deeper level, though, this book is really about *finding out what you love to do* and *making the decision to do it*. It's about moving to a place that you love.

In order to identify that place, we're going to explore your dreams, not just about business ownership, but relating to every aspect of your life. We're going to look at your past and see what it tells us when it comes to shaping your future. We're going to look at where you are right now—professionally, personally, in relation to the other people in your life—and we're going to uncover the path that will lead you to where you want to be.

Dreaming with Your Eyes Wide Open

Over the last several years I have worked with thousands of women—women in corporations, in their own businesses, in the universities, in the home—who were trying to make the same decision you are. Everywhere, there has been movement, internal and external transition, along with the desire for it and the fear of it. Everything, it seems, is in flux.

I have felt this myself, and I've seen it in others. And I have been struck by two things.

First, I've noticed that the idea of owning one's own business has become almost a universal proxy for finding what we love to do. If, finding yourself in a position that you hate, you think to yourself, "Well, maybe I should start my own business," then count yourself among the millions who are doing the same. There are many of us who are trying to leave lack of fulfillment behind, looking for something to jump into with both feet and call our own.

No one ever really taught *any* of us how to make decisions. Certainly, no one shared with us a process for finding out what we love to do. We have been taught to look to the outside to find the answer, to quickly grab hold of any likely alternative *out there*.

When I was a corporate executive I attended many, many management training sessions. I have been rock climbing, I have been hiking . . . in fact, I believe I've done just about every woodsy, outdoor-type, team-based problem-solving exercise in existence. I've sat in hotel and convention-center conference rooms from coast to coast, going through every indoor-type management seminar known to the corporate mind. And *never,* with all that work, did any of it ever focus on *me* and what *I* wanted to do with my life. I was never asked, and never given permission, to explore me.

This book offers a way for you to do just that: to explore what business ownership could mean for you—in reality, as an individual in unique circumstances with unique goals—and for you to judge your prospects for success before you bet the farm. It's a process that is designed to get you to the *right* place, not just a new place.

I'm not trying to get every woman (or every man) who reads this book to go out and start a business. Far from it. Business ownership is fun, exciting, rewarding . . . but it is also *tough*. Damn tough. A lot of people fail at it, and it's devastating when they do, both financially and personally.

One thing I can promise you, as we go through this experience together, is honesty. You are not going to hear countless pep talks from me. You are not going to read tale after tale of fabulous people who started out with $500 and built million-dollar empires. You already know those stories.

I believe those stories are good motivators. I also believe they encourage too many people to take the plunge—people who, for their own good, should never do so.

I am going to be brutally honest and direct and tell you that most people are just not cut out to be business owners. Over the past several years I've seen too many people jump right in, thinking all they needed was a dream. *It just ain't so.*

So if, after going through this process, you determine that business ownership is for you, then that's fantastic. If you say instead "not for me," then that's also fantastic. After all, business ownership is simply one choice.

And I emphasize: It's a *life* choice. But there are many possible life choices that can come out of this process. You might decide to change the way things are going in your present job. You might decide to go back to school. You might decide to end a relationship. There is literally no limitation to what could come out of this, as long as there is no limitation to your dreams.

The process set forth in this book can be a preparation for success in business; it can also be a way of avoiding business failure and preparing for success in some other area. Above all, it's a way of determining what, for you, would constitute a balanced life, a life that you choose.

At a certain point in her very successful career as an investment banker, Donna decided that the time had come for her to take the plunge and leave her corporate job to become a consultant. Again, she enjoyed much success. To make a long story short, the business grew quickly, and she was soon making a lot of money. It looked as if she had the bull by the horns and was on her way to living the dream life.

But it all went wrong. Almost immediately, Donna grew very unhappy, because, despite her success, there was one thing she could not deal with: uncertainty. No matter how well she was doing today, she couldn't stop worrying about tomorrow. Would her success be only temporary? How would she be doing in six months? The fear almost destroyed her, until she finally headed back to a life in which she was far more comfortable.

"What I really value," she told me, "is having the security that allows me to be happy, that lets me concentrate on enjoying every part of my life. Right now, I'm worrying all the time about what's coming next, and I just don't like it." End of story.

I don't think of Donna as a quitter, as someone who gave up. She *moved* up when she decided to do what was right for her. She moved up and moved on by doing a very brave thing: She looked at herself honestly.

When I was young I thought I wanted to be a nun. I wanted to enter the convent right out of eighth grade, but my father said "no way." I begged God to forgive him. I finally got my wish in 1971, the day after I graduated from high school.

After the very first day at Holy Family Convent in Manitowoc, Wisconsin, I knew I didn't want to be a nun. How could that be? I was devastated. I felt like I had just ruined my entire life.

I had spent so much time preparing to devote my life to this calling and now I knew, in one day, it wasn't for me. You can imagine how anxious I was to call my dad and tell him about my newest decision! It took a trip to Wisconsin, after years of dreaming about being a nun, to understand that I was in love with the *idea* of being a nun. What I loved was the respect the sisters got from the congregation. I loved that all the kids looked up to them. I loved the idea of wearing a habit that made it obvious to all that I was a good woman, a woman of God.

But I did not love at all what it took to get there. Poverty, chastity, and obedience were well beyond my personal capabilities, regardless of how much I loved the end result. I was in love with being it, not in love with doing it! And thus, my "calling" as a nun was short-lived.

It's easy to be dazzled by the trappings of business ownership. It's easy to fall in love with the notion that we have the greatest money-making idea ever. It's easy to spend a lot of time dreaming about what it will be like to be our own boss.

Overcoming the romance, the seduction, the promise, and finding out what you really like and want: Now, that's difficult. It's also just plain smart.

So if you're ready to rethink the old notions of "what it takes," then get ready for some hard work. You're not going to find any handy formulas here to tell you whether or not you can be a success. The process here will be introspective, subjective, beginning and ending with you, which is why it can work for you, no matter what your prior experience, no matter what your current circumstances.

Who This Book Was Written For

This book isn't just for women thinking of starting a business. It's for any woman who's already started one or inherited one. It's for any woman who has successfully established her business, but is now beginning to experience some of the same confusion, fatigue, even boredom, that came with working for others. It's for anyone who feels it's time to reassess what she wants from her professional life, her personal life, her life taken as a whole. It's for any woman in transition. It's for anyone who is ready to measure her dreams against her reality, in all its aspects—and to see if she can make that reality measure up to her dreams.

And that leads me to my last point. Even though this book was written from the perspective of a woman business owner who works with women business owners, this is an experience, a book, a process, that should be embraced by both women and men, including those in our corporations. What works for the individual *can* work for the corporation, to the benefit of all. For all our new language, from *reengineering* to *quality circles* to *skill-based pay,* in the final analysis any company's success is based on one simple thing: its people. Helping people, giving people permission to discover who they are and what they love to do, and then working with them to find that spot in the organization that is right for them, are, without equivocation, the efforts that will yield the highest payback for both the individual and the corporation.

My hope is that this experience will be a way for us all to help one another along, on what may be the most important journey any one of us will ever take. I challenge you to do the work for yourself. I also challenge you to give this opportunity to someone you work for, to someone who works for you, to someone you love, to someone who loves you. I challenge you to address the problem: that too many of us are doing work that we don't love doing.

Innerpreneuring

I can't emphasize it strongly enough: It's not the nuts and bolts, or access to material resources, or even the fundamental soundness of the business idea that determines success or failure. It's the quality of the person who's turning that idea into reality. And it's just the same in every other endeavor.

I wrote this book out of personal experience as a business owner—and as someone who has spent countless hours working with other business owners and prospective business owners, helping them to shape their own visions of why they were in business and what they wanted out of it.

I have a word for the approach to business ownership that you'll find expressed in this book. I call it *innerpreneuring:* creating a business from the inside out. It means focusing on you and you alone, because when you're looking into the option of going into business, the *first* thing you need to do is take a step back and look into *yourself.* After all, you are the founder.

Innerpreneuring means beginning with the person in the business and ending with the person in the business. It demands that we ask ourselves, first, what we are bringing to our ventures (in terms of *personal* resources, interests, and situation), and second, what we want and need.

To understand the concept of innerpreneuring requires adopting an expanded notion of what makes for a successful business, because for the innerpreneur there is no true success in business unless there is also a successful *life*. It's this comprehensive notion of success that makes the process outlined here work not only for future business owners but for anyone who is ready to make an inner-directed major life change.

The concept of innerpreneuring lies in every step in the decision-making process you are about to undertake.

I'll start off in Part I by giving you an idea of some of the key beliefs that underlie my approach to business ownership and the decision-making process itself. I'll also introduce some of the techniques and tools you'll be using on your journey of self-discovery.

Part II is that journey: You'll be looking at your current situation, your past experience, and your hopes for the future. You'll do exercises, alone and with others, that will give you a clearer view of where you've been, where you are, and who you are . . . and you'll use that view to shape a vision of the right future for you.

Finally, in Part III, we'll take that vision and form a concrete action plan for making it a reality. And it doesn't matter whether you'll have decided to start a business, to continue with one you're already running, or to go off in an entirely different direction: You are going to know exactly where you want to go, and why, and how to get there.

Throughout, I'm going to keep emphasizing that single core belief: that success depends on the individual, that the "soft stuff" (who you are, what you value, the quality of your spirit and your relationships) *is* the "hard stuff." You could know every management technique, have all the nuts-and-bolts information in the world, and none of it would be as important and *effective* in finding true success—*success in life*—as is knowing yourself.

My Promise to You

And now a final word before you get started. I will not promise to provide easy, quick answers for you, because there aren't any. I haven't found a miracle method that will get you to where you want to go quickly and easily.

What *will* you get from this experience, then? First and foremost, *you'll find that it's you who will provide the answers.* Only you can, after all. This book simply offers a process and method for helping you to do that.

If you are truly willing to invest the time and do the work to arrive at your own answers, I will promise you'll find:

- A high likelihood that you will discover what you really love to do
- A better understanding of who you are
- A sense of community
- Friendships
- Inspiration
- A boost in your courage to go forward
- An increased probability of success in whatever you choose to do
- An action plan for achieving your life choice

I won't promise you a miracle. Instead, I'll promise you this marvel: *You are going to find your path to becoming who you want to be.*

INC. YOUR DREAMS

INTRODUCTION: MY STORY

I PUT IN SIXTEEN years in Corporate America. From MBA to senior vice president, I was "on the inside."

I looked like I was on the inside. There was a time when there were just three colors in my closet: black, blue, and gray. In my dresser there were a hundred silk bow ties; every workday morning found me tying one of them on so perfectly that the few men who wore bow ties would routinely admire my skill.

I have to say it: I was the perfect executive employee, committed, self-motivated, working nights and weekends, sweating the details. I met every deadline, obsessed as I was with getting through my in-box and doing well. Each company I worked for received more than a fair return for every dollar it paid me.

I was willing to play the role and work hard because I enjoyed it and because it was necessary. I was part of a generation of businesswomen enjoying unprecedented opportunities in Corporate America. And through hard work, I smashed through the glass ceiling—maybe because I never internalized the fact that there *was* one, at least for me.

I worked for Revlon, Arthur Andersen, Citicorp, CompuCard, and a handful of other companies, garnering most of the distinctions of corporate success. I was a vice president, a senior vice president, a divisional president. I made more money than I'd ever dreamed possible. I had large staffs, controlled hefty yearly budgets, presented strategies to boards of directors, participated in high-level policy decisions. I had profit-and-loss accountability, that often nerve-wracking but much-sought sign of *real* power in the corporation, for most of my career.

Throughout my career, I'd passed every performance review with flying colors, although each report included comments like "outstanding performance but hard to control," "independent thinker," "creative, looks at things differently," "token entrepreneur," "emotional."

I didn't *think* like the perfect insider, didn't think "in the box"—and I spoke my mind when I thought differently. Never with inappropriate emotion, if you ask me, but often with passion because I cared. Maybe independence of mind and outspokenness didn't coincide with the ideal profile you might find in an employee-hiring guideline, but *I* knew that that was what made me truly valuable.

Ready for a New Direction

My superiors must have thought so too. In 1990, I was working outside Philadelphia for a division of a diversified financial services company worth $19.4 billion at the time, as a senior vice president of marketing. The CEO asked me to head up a new project: establishing an "intrapreneurial" entity, an independent company within the company. The goal was to create a new business and a new way of doing business.

The CEO had spent the past couple of years trying to fundamentally change the corporate culture of our billion-dollar company. A group of consultants had finally convinced him that he could not create the new out of the old. He had to start from scratch and set up a whole new entity.

He wanted me not only to head that entity but to design it from the ground up. He asked me to give up my position, my staff, all my current responsibilities, to take on the task of creating a brand-new company that would incorporate his vision of the future.

Why me? "Because," he replied, "you're the only entrepreneur in the company, and you'll go over any barrier to make something happen."

I was a bit leery of the assignment, to tell the truth. My first reaction was "I'm on my way to outplacement here. I'm a woman who's known for speaking her mind in a conservative, male-dominated corporation. I'm almost forty. Is this some very careful way of easing me out?" And even if they were serious, was the company really behind this idea? *I* was ready to follow through; were they?

My second reaction was fear, self-doubt. There I was, sitting in the CEO's office, being invited to head up the most daring project that this company had ever undertaken—and I still couldn't quite believe he was asking *me!*

I was very, very nervous, on many counts. But there were simply no two ways about it. I couldn't say "yes" fast enough. In a strange way, I had been preparing for this opportunity for the last twenty years. Scared but ready: That's where I was.

My boss gave me two parameters regarding what I needed to accomplish. First, I had to design and create a company that could produce sales of at least $500 million a year. Second, the business had to be relationship-based.

There was a lot of talk at the time in Corporate America about achieving relationship-based businesses. But my boss had a very specific, and rather intriguing, model in mind: *It's a Wonderful Life*. He told me to go back and watch the movie again. He said he wanted to build a company that related to individual customers exactly the way Jimmy Stewart's George Bailey related to his. We were going to do business with them on the basis of knowing them well and put our trust in the strength of their character as much as in the strength of their balance sheet.

I must have watched that movie at least ten times over the next couple of weeks, and the more I analyzed it, the more it made sense to me that what my boss was asking for *could be done*. If *I* could make it work, that is . . . and I was going to, no matter what. George Bailey was going to be proud.

From Insider to Intrapreneur

I was ready to roll, sitting at my desk, facing what I affectionately called my "blank sheet." Literally.

It was entirely up to me to identify a market, develop a plan for the service we would bring to that market, and sell the idea to our board of directors. I could no longer lean on any of the crutches that came with working in the organization: it was no longer a question of reviewing, critiquing, modifying, but of *creating*.

Suddenly I knew that there was a world of difference between the romance of entrepreneurship and entrepreneurship itself. This was the morning after the romance, when the hard work of building something *real* began. From a blank sheet of paper to a $500 million company: Could I do that? Where was our market?

From the beginning, I had an inkling. By day two of this new assignment, I knew I wanted to do something with women because, for the most part, their economic power was still invisible to Corporate America. I felt then, as I do now, that no company was doing a particularly good job of communicating with women and offering legitimate solutions to their real needs. I was certain that there were big opportunities for the company that could meet the needs.

I started doing research around the various segments of the women's market. There were any number of possible ways to go, but nothing clicked until I came across an article on women who were starting their own businesses.

I have to admit, that article really took me by surprise. The numbers quoted were *outrageous!* From 3 percent of businesses in this country owned by women in 1960 to a projected *50 percent* in the year 2000! Today, those statistics are much more familiar than they were as recently as 1990. At the time, it was hard even for me to believe that so many women were starting successful businesses, many of them on a pretty grand scale, and succeeding.

But I knew, the moment I finished that article, that *this* was the market we were going to serve. Further research bore me out, in spades. Not only was this a largely ignored market group, but these women were actually succeeding at a *higher rate* than their male counterparts.

This was big. I'd found it.

To make a long story short, I gathered my team together, and we moved quickly to set up our plan. We did all the standard stuff you do when you want to move into a market: sized it, ran demographic and financial analyses, learned all the statistics by heart, organized traditional focus groups.

We also started, every month, bringing in a couple of hundred women and not only picking their brains but asking them to open up their hearts to us. We asked them to share their innermost thoughts and feelings about what they were doing and what they wanted to do . . . and they did. We literally developed the business's central concepts along with them.

From Intrapreneur to Entrepreneur

I won't take the time to describe the company we formulated—with their help—in detail. Suffice it to say that, from the day we sent out our first press release, the reaction was phenomenal.

We never spent a dime on advertising. Our business was fueled entirely by word of mouth and media interest. We were widely hailed as the first for-profit corporation that was prepared to address the needs of the women business owners' market, including making capital available to them.

Our market responded immediately. From our very first offering—a personal yet practical seminar that would let women explore the option of business ownership—women called and sent in their checks. These women were *out there,* waiting for something like this.

They responded because we were ready to meet their needs in a way that had never been seen before. They responded because we offered them access to the tools and resources they needed to become successful. They recognized that we'd created a company for them that dealt directly with the most pressing problems women business owners face. It was a company that was created by successful women, most of whom were business owners, to serve successful women business owners.

We were different. Our market acknowledged that from the beginning. Women from all walks of life—teachers, corporate vice presidents, business owners, students, full-time moms—responded to our expanded notion of success, which integrated both the personal and professional dimensions of their lives. I recall one woman remarking, "This company has the brain of a for-profit and the soul of a not-for-profit."

Everything was going great. I loved what I was doing. I felt blessed every day, and I mean that in the deepest way.

I loved the women we were working with. I admired their energy and their accomplishments. Secretly, deep down, I wondered if I could do what they were doing with their lives.

Gradually, something happened to me: I found that I'd become so involved with, so close to the individuals I was meeting in this market that *I became one of them.*

By April 1993, though, I'd begun to hear rumblings from senior management that we might not be a good strategic fit with the parent company's other operations. If you've spent any time in Corporate America, you know that "not being a good strategic fit" can mean almost anything—but never anything positive. I knew we were in trouble.

Within a month—on May 7—*The Wall Street Journal* announced that the company was being quietly scuttled. We were too far afield from the parent company's core business. They didn't want to make loans to women business owners anymore.

We were written up in the national press. We were on the radio. We were invited to speak at functions all over the country. We were holding our training programs. We were developing a strong customer base. We were on our way to being the defining corporation for women business owners.

And they pulled the rug out from under us.

How could that be? When there was every indication that we were headed for success, how could they abandon this untapped market?

I've asked myself that question many times, and I've come to believe that it was exactly *because* we were so successful that the parent company suddenly pulled back. We'd managed to reveal a market whose size and aspirations no one had really comprehended before. The demand was there. It was real. And the parent company knew that if they stayed in this market, they were going to have to invest a significant amount of capital.

When we started out, we believed that the requests for financing would average $50,000 to $75,000. What we quickly discovered was that women had much bigger ideas, bigger dreams: They were creating businesses, but not small ones. They were creating businesses that were large and national and complex, and they needed capital well in excess of the averages we had projected. They were requesting $2.2 million and $700,000 and every amount in between.

But the parent company decided that they didn't want to invest the capital required to build this business. They decided that they didn't have the core competencies or the appetite for the commercial lending business. It was a legitimate business decision.

But I was destroyed inside. I can't really express what was torn out of me. They'd taken away something that I cared deeply about. I'd loved what I was doing in a way that I had never known before.

"So," I asked myself, "now what?" Should I find another corporate job?

I just couldn't get comfortable with that option. These women had become much more than statistics, much more than a market. They'd become real people, real faces, real lives to me. And they were suddenly back where they'd started, with no one to meet their needs in the way that we'd been prepared to.

So I made my decision. I divorced the corporation, which—I will not kid you—was not easy. All change is painful in some way.

I formed a new team to continue our work with women business owners. And together we accomplished the best thing I've ever done.

We created Capital Rose.

We created Capital Rose because women's needs are going unmet in the marketplace and because we believe we understand and can uniquely satisfy those needs. We created Capital Rose because we know more about women business owners and their unmet needs than about anything else. We created Capital Rose because meeting those needs is the thing we love to do.

Capital Rose is not a cause. We have no desire to be included in the "battle of the sexes." We did not create Capital Rose because women are "disadvantaged" and certainly not because they need to be subsidized in order to succeed. Women aren't a remedial group. They need access to the same help that any business owner needs.

We are problem-solvers. By addressing the most pressing problems faced by women business owners, we offer solutions that allow women to concentrate on building and growing their businesses. Ultimately, it means success at a faster rate.

The very first problem we set out to solve was access to capital. Historically, women have had more trouble than men in raising capital, regardless of the strength of their business plans. We decided that it was time to do something about this, that it was time to establish a source of capital that didn't rely on the whims of corporate strategy.

We decided that it was well within our collective power as women to amass a pool of capital for financing our businesses. Rather than meeting on it, talking about it, and hoping the government would solve the problem—rather than crying "foul"—we decided let's just do it.

And so we are doing it. We created the Capital Rose Perpetual Fund, a not-for-profit Pennsylvania corporation that is raising $40,000,000 to finance women-owned businesses. How? By asking women (and men), four million of them to be exact, to each contribute $10 to the Fund. It's a national effort. It's grassroots. And the Fund will last forever, perpetual in every sense of the word. It's a symbol of what we can accomplish when we work together—for ourselves, our children, our families, and our communities. The Fund represents women coming together around a central goal and co-opting economic influence. It is designed to be inclusive, to ensure that every woman can participate. Each small contribution from millions of women is a symbol of a twenty-first-century community of women, working together with a unified purpose.

We will continue to solve problems for the women business owner market. As we do, we'll continue to design and implement organizations that most effectively meet the needs of the market. When we created the Fund, we were adamant that it be a non-profit entity because we wanted to create a lasting symbol of the collaborative efforts of women. But we've also developed organizations that are for-profit. Capital Rose is dedicated to accelerating the success of women-owned businesses through access to financing, information, products, and services. Women who make money and know how to run a business want to conduct business with women who do the same. We serve the market of women business owners and aspiring women business owners. We best serve that market because we *are* the market!

And, we are sharing our knowledge and experience about the women's market with corporations throughout the United States in industries as diverse as manufacturing, financial services, consumer marketing, and professional services firms. Why? Because we believe that if we assist corporations in providing products and services that truly meet the real needs of women and women business owners, we are fulfilling our mission. We are helping to make women business owners real, visible, and economically important to corporations.

I expect this commitment by corporations to women and women business owners to continue and accelerate exponentially. I predict substantial amounts of capital and resources will be dedicated to communicating, understanding, learning, and developing products and services for women business owners. We are the market of the future. Five years ago, only a handful of corporations were interested in serving us; today, it is a rare company that is not committed to finding a way to recognize our achievements, numbers, and the economic power we wield.

We think this is very important work and ultimately yields access to all the tools and resources required for success.

We are doing what we love and we love what we're doing. We're looking to contribute. We're building legacies for our families, our colleagues, our communities. We're acting on our right to self-reliance. We're seeking dignity.

I believe that those are goals that all of us can reach, in any walk of life. For some of us, business ownership is the choice for attaining them. For others, the answer lies elsewhere. What matters is that each of us finds her way and that we all move forward together.

PART I

Getting Ready for the Trip

1

It's Not the Idea, It's You

HAVE YOU EVER seen those lists that describe "The Ten Traits of Successful People"? I know you have; they're in just about every magazine that you pick up these days. As soon as you put together a list of success traits that's supposedly all-encompassing, what you have is the lowest common denominator—and the successful individuals I have met are far from the lowest common denominator.

Over the past several years, I have reached some conclusions about business ownership, business owners, and life that now form the basis of a belief system. I'd like to share with you some of what I've learned. The following seven key beliefs are the underpinnings of the process that you are undertaking, and you'll be hearing echoes of them throughout this book.

Belief #1: Every Success Is Unique

A couple of years ago I attended the Inc. 500 Conference, an annual three-day event sponsored by *Inc.* magazine for the men and women who own and run the 500 fastest-growing companies in the United States.

It was entrepreneur heaven. Energy, passion, and zest for life were everywhere. These people *believed in themselves*. For me they were magnetic . . . and I was walking-on-air inspired, for three straight days. Being there as a guest among the chosen, I had a sense of our greatness, of our ability to create our own futures.

Each of the 500 was unique. Some of them had come up with a business plan and then set about making it work, while others had struggled for years to get where they wanted to be. For some, business was an end in itself; for others it was a means to an end, like the person who used the profits from his business to fund a minority orchestra. If you heard one story, you definitely had not heard them all. There were 499 more to go.

I looked, listened, carefully observed. . . . Hard as I tried, I could not come up with anything that tied them all together.

And I saw clearly, for the first time, that successful business owners are really a bunch of exceptions to the rule. Anita Roddick, founder and president of the Body Shop, is right on when she says, "There is no scientific answer for success. You can't define it. You've got to live it and do it."

So if you are looking for an aptitude test for business ownership from me . . . sorry. If you are looking for a list of attributes to tell you whether you are "the type" . . . sorry again.

We can't get around the simple fact that we're different in terms of our DNA, our upbringings, our current situations, and our dreams; our businesses are going to be different too. So what it's going to take for each of us to get there will be different.

We *all* have the right stuff, if we decide we want to use it. We can only use it, though—I'm convinced—when we find what it is that we love to do. *That's* when we decide to call on the right stuff within us, because there's no longer any choice in the matter.

Some people are lucky enough to know what they love from the start. Others diligently seek it out. Still others find themselves in an unexpected situation that brings forth a sense of "That's it!" However we find it, though, when we *do* find it, we discover that we *do* have the right stuff. Loving what you do opens the door.

That's something a list will never do, and that's why I find lists to be confining. They start defining who we are and what we are capable of doing before we've had a chance to discover what it is we want to do with our lives. They do not help us expand our definition of ourselves. Rather than being building blocks, "prerequisite characteristics" can become barriers that keep you from finding what it is you love to do.

Evaluating your ability to achieve success—as a business owner or in anything else—involves looking at *yourself,* your inner self. You must create your own list.

The writer Gertrude Stein once said, "Let me listen to me and not to them." When I came across that quote, I put it up on my refrigerator. Every morning as I pour the coffee, I'm reminded to make that my motto for the day. Perhaps you will make it yours, too.

Belief #2: It's Not the Idea, It's You

I don't think there is a person alive who hasn't sat at the kitchen table with a family member or friend and talked about a great idea they have. You've done it, I'm sure, and you know that in those conversations there's a wonderful sense of excitement, of what could be. It's *fun* to talk about creative, new ideas.

I bet you've heard this one, too: "I can't believe it, they stole my idea! I knew I was right!"

Then there's this one. Present a simple, obvious idea to someone and you are likely to hear, "Why hasn't anyone else ever thought of this?" When you hear this comment, stand clear, because the answer is "Someone has."

Good ideas do not make a business. They aren't even especially important to success. In fact, having a good idea is the best *wrong* reason to start a business, because good ideas are false gods. They make for great beginnings, but lousy endings.

There's nothing unique about having an idea. In the life of every idea, it's longevity that counts, and that's entirely determined by the hands that hold it, mold it, and do something with it. Conception alone offers no particular advantage.

I personally took something like five hundred calls last year from women across the country, and each conversation started with "Rebecca, let me tell you my idea." Before I had a chance to take a breath, the caller would jump in, describe in great detail her idea for a business, and at the end ask, "Rebecca, you hear a lot of ideas, what do you think of mine? Is it one of the better ones you've heard?"

Just about all of these callers were *shocked* to hear me say that I had absolutely *no interest* in the idea. Not at that stage.

What I'm interested in, pure and simple, is the caller . . . her family . . . her relationship to herself, to her immediate world, and the world at large. If you want my opinion on your chances of making a go at business ownership, I need to know about *you,* because you are the ultimate predictor of your success.

Sometimes it's bad ideas, or at least what most people *think* are bad ideas, that lead to the fairy-tale endings. Take Dr. Seuss: Thirty-seven publishers rejected his idea of the kind of books he wanted to write before he sold his first one. Jim Henson was rejected by all the major networks in the United States before he found someone in England who believed in him. And how many people thought Anita Roddick was completely nuts to deny herself, because of her principles, resources that other cosmetic companies relied upon?

I have seen great ideas butchered in the hands of the wrong person, and I have seen simple, obvious, even downright uninspiring ideas turned into real barn-burners in the hands of the right person. Great ideas don't make great businesses, people make great businesses. This is one of those truths that everyone seems to accept as right on target . . . then completely ignores.

Another example is Scott Cook. As president of Intuit, he was responsible for bringing to market the personal financial software called Quicken. In the early days, people thought that Cook's plan was "stupid" and he was turned down by some of the finest venture capital firms in the country. At one point, Intuit was struggling to pay its telephone bills and movers carted away office furniture because of overdue accounts. Nonetheless, he persevered . . . for nine years. The result? He'll earn $338 million on the sale of his company to Microsoft.

The fact is, everyone has great ideas. Most people never lift a finger to act on them. That's where the difference lies. I have often said that I'd rather invest in the right person and a mediocre idea, any day, than in the wrong person and the best idea I've ever heard. *It's not the idea, it's you.*

If that's true—people, not ideas, make great businesses—then starting with the notion that the idea can carry us to success is effectively starting *in the middle of the process.* There aren't many activities in life where you can start in the middle, forgoing the first steps, and end up with something that works well. You can't build a house that way. You can't build a career that way. In fact, start in the middle on most anything, and it's almost a sure bet that you will eventually have to scrap the effort and start all over.

Belief #3: You Are What You Choose

It really does come down to you. That can be so easy to forget. We often say we believe such things, but somehow we don't feel them. Then, every so often, life meets you halfway. It offers the opportunity to see all over again that the things you believe in are more than mere words. I know that's what happened to me.

It was September 1993: the twentieth, to be exact. My partners and I were in New York. We'd just made a presentation to a prospective corporate sponsor, and were now going to meet my agent and good friend, Ling, to celebrate her birthday.

By the time we met in the Oak Room of the Plaza Hotel, everyone was talking at the same time. Our friend, impatient to know how the meeting had gone, bombarded us with endless questions, and we just as eagerly provided her with answers, reflections, feelings—all at the same time.

After a while, the cacophony of satisfied voices began to subside. Our energy was spent. We had celebrated our success—our business success—and now it was time to celebrate *life,* to celebrate our friend's birthday. We moved without a hitch from business to our personal lives, to our friendships. In a seamless, completely connected way, it all mattered deeply to us. It all counted.

So, it was out with the cards and well wishes, the peanuts and the chardonnay. Life is a gift we give to each other. Without friends, what would the rest of it be worth? Would any of the rest of it have the same meaning? I didn't think so. Sitting there, even though I hadn't earned a single dime that day, I felt as blessed and as rich as I ever have.

Suddenly, Ling reached over and took one of my partners' hands and said, "Oh, let me read your palms." We looked at one another. This was a talent that we didn't know about. Our friend reads palms! She told us that her mom had taught her and that her family had been doing it for hundreds of years.

For the first time, the table was quiet. There is something very exciting about a person who can tell you something about yourself, your future. We leaned forward to hear what our partner's palms said about her life, in anticipation of our own readings.

I went last, presenting my right hand. Ling looked at it and didn't say a word. Was that a bad sign? Then she looked at me and said, "Let me see the hand you were born with."

"What?"

"Let me see the left hand. The left hand shows what you were born with."

I put out my left hand, and she explained. "The lines, indentations, imprints on the left hand show the palmist what you were born with. Where you started from. Your situation, your 'initial portfolio' of abilities, talents, and temperaments. The right hand shows what you've done with what you were given."

I was struck hard by that explanation. In fact, I was so struck by it that I honestly don't remember anything she said about what she saw in my palms.

All I could think was "Two hands, one life." The phrase popped into my head immediately. There was something about looking at my hands and realizing, maybe for the first time, that I am the architect, designer, and builder of my own life. It brought it home for me.

On the drive back to Philadelphia, I sat in the backseat. It was dark by then, and I must have looked at my hands fifty times as passing traffic provided flashes of illumination. Were they really different, these two hands? Was the right hand always in transition? Always adding or subtracting lines and length and depth, depending on how I chose to live my life? The left hand was fixed in time. Maybe at birth? Maybe before? But this right hand, now that was a work-in-progress. I was the creator of this one.

This idea had a profound impact on me. I'm not even sure that I believe in palmistry. It doesn't matter. For me, it became a metaphor for helping me to see and feel my own power. This new view of my hands, of me, has become a living symbol of something that I'd only thought I knew.

We are not fixed in time and space. What we are born with is only the beginning—the pencil rendering of a vision; we add the color, the texture, the paint. We sign the masterpiece. In the end, it belongs to us. We have created it.

Two hands, one life. Your two hands together hold all the cards you will play in the ultimate game. The game is short. Each play counts. Each play is recorded on your right hand, and you are the only one who can choose what will be written there.

Successful people don't just fall into being successful. They create their success—one choice at a time.

Life is about choices. You are what you choose.

Belief #4: Invest in Yourself

The vice president of market research for a Fortune 500 cosmetics company told me about a focus group his company conducted. A variety of women were being quizzed on how they spent their days while he watched from behind a two-way mirror. The participants were talking freely, answering questions posed by the moderator, providing lots of feedback . . . until they were asked, "What do you do each day for yourself?" To his amazement, the entire room fell silent. These women were so busy doing for others that they could not come up with *one* thing they did for themselves each day.

He still couldn't believe it. I could.

Someone once described women as "emotional service stations." Not the most elegant image, but pretty accurate. We provide other people with the fuel they need. We do our best to fix what's gone wrong and offer service with a smile.

There's certainly nothing wrong with that. We should be proud of our strength to give so much. But we forget (and here's what *is* wrong) to value *ourselves*.

I don't see the demands that come with our lifestyles easing up anytime soon. We are building futures, for ourselves and others: trying to climb the corporate ladder or creating businesses while keeping the home fires burning, nurturing our relationships with friends and family, raising our kids, and, in many cases, starting to realize that we will be grandparents in the not so distant future. I get tired just thinking about all the things we cram into our lives!

If I told you that in order for your new business to succeed, you needed to invest in new computer equipment, you would do it without much hesitation. If I told you that in order to get the next promotion, you needed to write a fantastic hundred-page report, you'd get right down to it. But if I tell you that to be successful in life, in your new business or wherever it is that you're headed, you have to start making an investment in yourself, why is it that you'll probably say, "I know," and then do nothing?

I can already hear you saying, "You're right, but . . ." There are no ifs, ands, or buts about this one! *You have to learn how to invest in yourself.*

The first step, then, is to give yourself *permission* to invest in yourself. Giving yourself permission means deciding that you are worth it. It means being ready to forgive yourself, too, especially in the beginning. Don't be too hard on yourself when you don't live up to your plans, and don't give up on the commitment. You'll fail sometimes, but it doesn't matter. The important thing is to keep trying.

What I am saying is quite simple: Give yourself the same kind of loving, careful attention you bestow on others. Don't try to find time for yourself, *make* time for yourself.

Begin now by *making a commitment to this process.* Promise yourself that you are going to expend all the time and energy it takes to explore yourself and find what it is that you love to do, as a step towards creating the life you want to lead. The quiet investments, the ones that make us who we are, prepare us to succeed.

No matter how busy you are, no matter how difficult it's been in the past for you to find ways to *consistently* invest in yourself, do it. You won't be the only one who's better off for it; all those people who rely on you as their "emotional service station" will benefit too. The more personally fulfilled you are, the more certain you are that you're heading where you want to be, the more you will have to give to others.

Belief #5: Do It Yourself; Don't Do It Alone

There's doing it alone, and then there's doing it yourself. There's a world of difference between the two.

When contemplating a big life decision like starting your own business, you want to own it, you want to design it in your own image. That's as it should be. The mistake we too often make, though, is confusing the need to call it ours with the necessity of doing it alone. In fact, if you start out with the notion that you are going to do it alone, I believe you greatly increase your probability of failure.

None of us should do it alone, and none of us really wants to do it alone. But we've been told for so long that that's the way it happens that we've become afraid to express what we are really feeling. How can you admit you may need someone else to do it with when the success stories are filled with those *incredible* (that is, not to be believed) entrepreneurs who make it against all odds? To say "I really would like to do this with someone else" is tantamount to admitting that you aren't a *super-entrepreneur.*

Well, if you're going to start a business, you should admit it. You'll feel better. You'll do better. In reality, no one does it alone, even though we sometimes like to think we do. The CEO doesn't. The business owner doesn't. The entrepreneur doesn't. The athlete doesn't. Oprah Winfrey doesn't.

> *An entrepreneur is someone willing to go out on a limb, having it cut off behind her, and discovering she had wings all the time.*
>
> Leigh Thomas, President
> Women's Radio Network Corp.

The lone hero, the single person who makes it all happen, is a *myth.* The reality is that there *is* no superhuman entrepreneurial type. There is no leader who stands above all others. There is always one individual who is out in front, of course: the star. But I know, and I think we all know, that person is not doing it alone.

Which isn't to say that business ownership, if that is your ultimate choice, isn't going to take you down the loneliest path in the world—because that's exactly where it could be taking you, even if you have a business partner. There isn't a business owner alive who hasn't stayed up most of the night, more than once, wondering if things were going to turn out okay. Those early-morning vigils are *gut-wrenching,* and no one can protect you from them.

Not too long ago, I wrote in my diary:

> Entrepreneurs commit themselves to the unreasonable and unknown, without sufficient resources or knowledge, without guarantees or assurances, with only a belief in themselves and those around them. They bushwhack into the woods not because they have to but because they want to.

Ah, to be so free. So crazy. Like an animal that trusts in its own ability to find food and shelter.

I did not choose to be an entrepreneur. But when I looked inside me, I saw, to my delight and horror, I was one.

Delight? Horror? Yes, because I definitely felt free, but I also suddenly felt alone. And feeling alone zaps my strength.

Anyone who's gone through a start-up can regale you with horror stories about all the things that go wrong. The horror stories are basically the same: They're not so much about handling difficult situations as they are about handling *oneself.* Nine times out of ten, it's not the situation itself that presents the real danger; the business challenges, the strategic challenges, the financing challenges will all pale in comparison to *the challenge presented by your own emotions.*

Managing your way through the emotional roller-coaster will be your most difficult challenge. That's why, to succeed, you must focus on yourself, and above all, believe in yourself. It's also why we must believe in ourselves, *together,* and know that we can rely on one another to share your successes and your failures.

Belief #6: You Get What You Measure

I ALWAYS WANTED TO BE SOMEBODY. NOW I REALIZE I SHOULD HAVE BEEN MORE SPECIFIC.

—LILY TOMLIN'S "BAG LADY"

If we don't have a clear idea of what we want, it's extremely difficult to know how to spend those 1,440 minutes we have each day. If we do not have specific goals in mind, we are burning energy without creating matter.

Goals drive action. *Measurable* goals drive accomplishment.

It's only logical. Take the company you work for: If it decided that the success of the company—and your raise—depended on sales volume, you would focus your energy on sales, not team-building. If your bonus depended on net profits, you would probably focus on cost-cutting, not on innovation. In other words, you and your fellow employees are going to try like hell to deliver what's being *measured.* It wouldn't make sense to work hard to accomplish things that aren't being measured, would it?

How do you make this idea—that you get what you measure—work for you? You start at a very basic level, taking each of your goals, and you work to express them with great specificity.

Many of us have goals such as "I want to be happy," "I want to be rich," "I want to retire," "I want to move," "I wish I had more time." These aren't really goals. They are dreams—and as long as they remain vague dreams, they are probably never going to be realized.

Accomplishment of your goals is tied directly to their level of specificity and your ability to measure movement toward them. I am absolutely convinced that you do, and can always, get what you measure, *as long as there is a clear, concrete measurement.*

Consequently, as we go through this decision-making process together, I am going to be a real taskmaster in asking you to define very specifically what it is that you want and how you are going to measure your results. I understand that you may *not* know exactly what you want right now. And that's exactly what we're going to be working on defining, step by careful step.

The power to get what you measure comes with grasping the details, not the big picture. No one goes directly from big dreams, big goals, to achievement.

Let me give you an example of the kinds of steps we need to take. I was working with a friend and I asked her, "What do you want out of life?" She said what she really wanted was to make her mother happy, and for her mother to be proud of her. But when I asked her how she would know she had reached her dream, she said, "I don't know. I guess I'll just know, won't I?"

I kept pushing my friend to be as specific as possible. Finally, she said, "I'll know when my mother can be with me." My friend lives in the United States. Her mother lives in Singapore. Reaching her goal means making it possible for her mother to come live with her.

Now we were getting somewhere. We'd gone from a vague goal ("I want to make my mother happy") to a specific description of what things will look like when she reaches that goal ("My mother will be in the United States, living with me"). And having that specific description made the goal suddenly much more easy to work toward.

The next step was determining the critical success factors. What has to go right for her to get her desired end result?

Her first response was "We both have to stay alive!"

True enough, so there's a timing aspect, considering her mother's age. One critical success factor becomes being able to bring her mother to live with her within, say, five years. Others are her mother meeting immigration requirements, my friend being in a financial situation to support her mother, and the two finding a place to live that can accommodate both of them.

You can see that there are several things that have to happen before my friend can reach her goal. So the last thing we did together was to define the steps that she needs to take. These included everything from familiarizing herself with immigration laws to making specific adjustments in her budget and lifestyle that will allow her to accelerate her savings toward a new house, and more. It's a long list, and she's got a lot to accomplish in the coming years, but by going from a vague goal to a specific vision of the fulfillment of that goal, my friend is now on her way to realizing her dream.

It's not just in the realm of personal dreams that we have to work to overcome our tendency to vagueness, however. We tend to get a little too lofty in our professional lives, too. I once worked with a guy who would always say, after we'd spent days drawing up elaborate strategies, "What are we going to do on Monday morning?" I loved that line. Can't you just hear him saying to the CEO, "Yeah, I hear all the concepts, good concepts, *but what are we going to do on Monday morning?*" Very good question.

He was really saying, "Okay, we've had our fun with all this dreaming and strategizing. Now, how are we going to start making it happen, and keep making it happen, step by tiny step?"

I've been there repeatedly, and I can tell you that the planning, the strategizing—the dreaming—*is* the fun part. It's a blast. It's incredibly invigorating, even when it involves a lot of work. But it always comes down to Monday morning, and what you're going to do when you hit the ground. Are you going to hit it running? And in which direction?

We are all surrounded by opportunity. The great ideas are there to be found. The plans for capitalizing on them are there to be made. But it's specific steps that carry us forward. You get what you do. You get what you measure.

Belief #7: It's Not for Everyone

There's one final belief that I'd like to share with you. Up until now, we haven't really talked specifically about business ownership. I think it's critical, though, to explore what it is and what it isn't.

Owning your own business is the American dream. It would be great: freedom, wealth, no constraints. Captain of your own ship. No more crazy bosses. It's got a lot of appeal to it, doesn't it? Ask a hundred people like yourself if they want to own their own business someday, and two thirds will give you a spirited thumbs-up.

Seeing past the romance, seduction, and promise is difficult. But that's exactly what we have to do.

Supposedly, no one knows how business ownership really works, or what it takes, until they've stepped into it. Supposedly, it's a mystery that "you can't really understand" until you experience it.

I think that's 100 percent incorrect. I believe that we can and must explore the realities of owning a business and sort through the rightness of the decision before putting everything on the line.

Almost every other profession I know has a formalized process for determining whether or not a person fits into that profession *before* she bets the farm. Sometimes, just knowing about the process is enough to keep us from making the mistake of entering a profession that isn't right for us.

Take medicine, for example. Lots of us would like to earn a doctor's salary. But when we think about becoming a doctor we don't see just the rewards: we can also clearly see what it takes to get there.

I know that to become a doctor it will take four years of college, four years of medical school, internship, residency—not to mention intelligence, skill, the stamina to remain on call for forty-eight hours at a stretch, and the stomach to deal with blood, cadavers, and a couple hundred thousand dollars' worth of debt. Now that's a pretty good reality check on my dream of becoming a doctor. I have to absolutely want to do all that before I even begin.

> *Some things have to be believed to be seen.*
>
> Lynn Yeakel, Candidate, 1994, U.S. Senate

I think that's why, tough as it is to become a doctor, there's a much higher success rate in that profession than you find in business creation.

Because business ownership has been romanticized in this culture, many of us are in love with the idea, but not the reality, of doing it. That's why there needs to be a way to go from the dream of business ownership to what you might call its virtual reality without going all the way *into* the reality. There needs to be a process that increases our chances of making the right decision.

Successful business creation starts at home. It begins with knowing you, your family, your friends, and what you want out of life. I asked one business owner how she made sure that the decision to go into it was the right choice for her. She said, "I took a pause. I reflected on me."

If business ownership is your dream, then you, too, should be giving well-grounded, serious consideration to making it real and not just dreaming. Understanding yourself and your world increases the likelihood of your success. I believe this process will move you in that direction.

This process isn't just about earning a living. It's about making *in-*

formed life choices. It's about you and what you want to be when you grow up. It's important to stay focused on the process itself and not to try to force your way toward one conclusion or another.

Keep an open mind, and accept from the start that business ownership might not be right for you. It's not right for everyone. Go into it accepting that possibility, and you can be sure that whatever decision you make, whatever life choice you make, you'll be making it with your eyes wide open. You'll have given yourself the best possible shot at doing the thing that's right for you.

"Dear Rebecca . . ."

Before we start our work together, I want you to sit down and write me a letter. I want you to get into the habit of exploring what is inside you in great detail. That's what the exercises in this book are going to ask of you, over and over again. This letter is a way of warming up, of providing yourself with a reference point.

So, here's what I'd like you to tell me: What do you want out of life? And how will you know when you get it?

These are very big questions, I know, and it will take some serious thought for you to formulate detailed answers that truly reflect your highest aspirations. Remember, you get what you measure.

If you have trouble getting started, ask yourself some further questions to help flesh out your dreams. Ask yourself: How am I feeling? Is anything missing in my life? Do I love how I spend my days? What does success mean to me?

Once you are done, send the letter with a self-addressed stamped envelope to me at Capital Rose, P.O. Box 1310, Malvern, PA 19355-0650, Attn.: Dear Rebecca.

When I receive the letter, I'm not going to read what you wrote. I am going to do something much more valuable for you. I am going to hold on to your letter and send it back to you in six months.

Why? So that, six months from now, you will be able to see what a difference the process you're about to undertake has made in helping you to achieve your dreams.

It just may be that in six months you'll have built an entirely new dream for yourself, for your life. Or perhaps your dream will be the same, only more specific, and more achievable because of it. In either case, by committing to the process in this book, you will have given shape and substance to your dreams and identified the steps you need to get there.

Right Information, Wrong Emphasis

I know that the focus I'm developing here with these key beliefs—with my whole approach to business ownership—runs contrary to the conventional wisdom. I know this is not the sort of advice that you, as a business owner or prospective business owner, are likely to find out there. Most people would tell you, for instance, that the idea is everything: that it's having the right idea at the right time and in the right place that makes for a great business.

In your excitement about the prospect of transforming your life, the process I'm asking you to undertake might make you a little impatient. You may be saying, "This is the soft stuff. I'm beyond that. I want hard facts. I want to move forward and find an accountant, get a good lawyer, write my business plan. This is a waste of time."

There are a lot of people out there waiting to capitalize on that kind of understandable impatience. They'll offer you the "Ten Traits." They'll show you how to get a business up and running in thirty days. They'll lay out all the "nuts and bolts" involved. And you will, eventually, have to know all the nuts and bolts, no question—but you shouldn't start there.

You can always learn what you don't know, and the how-to stuff you are more than capable of learning. That "hard stuff" is the *easy*

stuff. You'll realize that after about two days into running your own business. In all my experience with women business owners, I cannot come up with one example, one anecdote, of a woman who failed because she couldn't master the how-to part. Not one.

The individual results of these business owners had little or nothing to do with their understanding of the nuts and bolts of business. I could relate stories of mistakes—some were costly mistakes, but none were in the final analysis the cause of a business's failure. The difference in outcomes depended on how well each individual had internalized one simple fact: that success or failure hinges on the ability to deeply understand, "It's not the idea, it's me."

The person who takes on the challenge, who implements the idea, who applies the nuts and bolts will account for 95 percent of the outcome. That means you.

Seven Key Beliefs

- ▲ *Every Success Is Unique*
- ▲ *It's Not the Idea, It's You*
- ▲ *You Are What You Choose*
- ▲ *Invest in Yourself*
- ▲ *Do It Yourself; Don't Do It Alone*
- ▲ *You Get What You Measure*
- ▲ *It's Not for Everyone*

2

Getting Ready for the Trip

ON THE JOURNEY we're going to take together, the excitement and the challenge come from trying to see with new eyes: seeing what we haven't seen before, in ourselves and in those around us. We tend to develop "blinkers" as we go through life—like racehorses that are only allowed to look straight ahead so they won't be distracted by the things they're not supposed to see—screening out certain perceptions or emotions simply as one way of getting through the day.

On this journey, I'll ask you to suspend judgment about what you are supposed to see, to let go of your ideas about what you want or *don't* want to see, and just *see;* if you're going to find within yourself the keys to your future success and happiness, then you've got to ditch those blinkers. The writer John Steinbeck once expressed very eloquently how important it is to do just that:

> It occurs to me to wonder and to ask how much I see or am capable of seeing. . . .
>
> Some years ago the U.S. Information Service paid the expenses of a famous and fine Italian photographer to go to America and to take pictures of our country. . . . The man had travelled

> everywhere in America, and do you know what his pictures were? Italy. In every American city he had unconsciously sought and found Italy. The portraits—Italians; the countryside—Tuscany and the Po Valley and the Abruzzi. His eye looked for what was familiar to him and found it. This is interesting as an incident, but I think we all do it. This man did not see the America which is not like Italy, and there is very much that isn't. And I wonder what I have missed in the wonderful trip to the south [of Israel] I have just completed. Did I see only America? I confess I caught myself at it. Travelling over those breathtaking mountains and looking down at the shimmering deserts, cut to wadis by the occasional flash floods, I found myself saying or agreeing—yes, that's like the Texas panhandle—that could be Nevada, and that might be Death Valley. The frightening thought . . . is that they weren't any of those places. They were themselves. But by identifying them with something I knew, was I not cutting myself off completely from the things I did not know, not seeing, not even recognizing, because I did not have the easy bridge of recognition? . . .
>
> This is a serious thing and it extends in many directions. Because we do not use quarter tones in music, many of us do not hear them in oriental music. How many people, seeing a painting, automatically dislike it because it is not familiar? And, most important of all, how many ideas do we reject without a hearing simply because our experience pattern can bring up no recognition parallel?

Are you seeing "America"? Or, like that photographer, are you seeing "Italy" because that's all you're prepared to see?

That's a question that you have to keep asking yourself: Am I seeing what I always see, or am I seeing something new? You need to completely rethink how you approach the opportunities that lie waiting in the landscape before you, and that has to begin and end with seeing things as they are, not how you want them to be.

THE MOMENT YOU ALTER YOUR PERCEPTION OF YOUR SELF AND YOUR FUTURE, BOTH YOU AND YOUR FUTURE BEGIN TO CHANGE.

—MARILEE ZDENEK

The purpose of this journey is for you to decide what you really want to do with your life. This is the hardest question any of us ever faces, so we're going to start out slowly, taking in all of the sights along the way, then gradually pick up speed as you lock into your destination.

You are going to determine the right destination. I'm just here to help, by leading you through some exercises my colleagues and I have developed over the years. The journey is the same for all of us; it's the destinations that are unique because each one of us finds hers within herself.

There are two "paths" on this journey, and you're going to travel them simultaneously. One leads outward, where you'll meet people who will provide a mirror in which you can see yourself anew. Because the journey *is* the same for all of us, it's a journey we can—and should—share. This is the part of the process where we make sure that you don't do it alone, and I'll be introducing it in the next chapter.

The other path leads inward. It involves going to a place where we seldom go. It involves learning to be. And because everything does begin and end with *you,* that's the path we're going to set off on first.

Before we go any further, I want you to put this book down and go shopping. Yes, every trip worth taking starts at the shopping mall!

Go out and buy yourself a journal, a notebook, or a diary. It can be any kind you like, whatever you are comfortable with, but buy something nice, something that says "you" all over it. With lots of room, too: room to write, to scribble, to draw, to paste things in. (And make sure it's a *new* notebook—don't just use one that's lying around the house; this is a new adventure, after all!)

Some parts of your journey are going to take place right in those pages, as you work through various exercises. And because the key to finding the right destination lies in your own thoughts and feelings, you're going to record *all* of your reactions, as you travel both the inward and outward paths. Your notebook is going to become a best friend.

So let's say good-bye for now while you put this book away and go meet that friend. We'll get together again once you have your notebook and are ready to go.

READY? GREAT, let's get started!

Let's start turning inward. Open your notebook, and thoughtfully answer this question:

Why are you reading this book?

"Obviously, because I'm thinking about starting a business." Okay, that's the short answer. But since this is a process that assumes you're still just *looking* at your options, you must be reading this book because you're not yet entirely sure that business ownership is the right choice for you.

> *Never dismiss your inner voice; it's that "mere feeling" that protects your essence and propels you towards true fulfillment.*
>
> Marcia Brodsky, Ph.D.

Perhaps you long for the freedom, yet are scared to death of the reality. Some days, business ownership seems to be the absolutely perfect answer. Others, it doesn't look right at all. You just don't have everything quite worked out yet, do you?

There's certainly nothing wrong with that. It's a big step you're considering, and you can *go crazy* trying to measure all the pros and cons!

Believe me, I've been there. I know you're feeling now like you have so many questions, and very few answers. Not to worry. The questions are your guideposts along the way. Without questions there would be no movement. In fact, the more questions you have, the better.

So let's just start by taking a shot at putting all those questions, all the contradictory thoughts and emotions that have been driving you crazy, down on paper. As you write, try to forget about the pros and cons of the matter. We'll have plenty of time for those later; for now, I want you to just let go, and dump all of your feelings of uncertainty, desire, hope, guilt, despair, confusion, and anticipation right into your journal. Concentrate on how you are *feeling*.

Now, put this book down. Really think deeply about why you're reading it, and start writing: "I am reading this book because . . ." When you're done, come on back.

Journaling and All That Scrap

ALL SERIOUS DARING STARTS FROM WITHIN.

—EUDORA WELTY

Now that you've blackened your first pages, I want to talk a bit about the art of journaling. I also want to try my hardest to convince you to learn how to do it well and to do it regularly. That's my agenda, and it's not hidden.

There are entire books devoted to the subject of journaling. I have never so much as cracked the cover of one of them. I have participated in more seminars than I care to remember, and whenever I heard the word journaling, I went numb. I went through the motions, as you may have done just now, because deep inside me I could not see the point.

I was a hard sell. No doubt about it. If anyone had ever told me that I would write a book one day and include journaling in it—in fact, promote it—I would have questioned that person's sanity. But it's funny how life has a way of sneaking up on you and . . . POW! you change.

I changed because I discovered that writing is the most powerful way I know of to sort through all the inner voices. I discovered that writing in my journal helped me to see me in a way that conversation alone could not. I changed because it works.

My journal is a reflection, and a pretty darn good one, of me. It's a picture. It has color. It holds my life.

My journal has lots of writing in it, but it contains a lot of other things as well. I doodle all over it. I put special pictures in it, tickets to events that I enjoyed, the slips of paper from fortune cookies, bows from special gifts, remembrances of new seasons and old ones. It is my memory, my best friend, and the keeper of my dreams for the future. I would be lost without it.

I write down things others have said, too, things that I want to remember and make part of my life. And, yes, my journal has clippings. Clippings galore! Clippings! Clippings! More clippings!

Come on, admit it, I know you're a clipper too. I have no idea why we are such prolific clippers, but I do know we love to clip. Maybe it's a way for us to hold on to our past. Or to create a path to the future. Clippings are about where we have been and where we want to go. They are about those things that have touched us. They are about hope . . . learning . . . change. They do belong in your journal.

So, what finally got me to start writing in a journal? Well, a couple of things. First, I got old enough, and my mother got old enough, for her to want to clear her attic of all those things she'd been lugging around for years, waiting to give to me. On one of her visits to my farm, she brought my baby book and some old scrapbooks I had put together as a kid.

For a while after she had left them with me, they sat together with all the other stuff I was going to look at when I had a free moment. As you can well imagine, that means they were pretty dusty by the time I got around to looking at them. But when I did, I saw that they held magic.

As I paged through the books, I was overcome by this incredible feeling of peace. I was rediscovering the me of the past. I could revisit the love that was offered to me, see it reflected in my eyes and in how someone had painstakingly recorded every pound I gained, every inch I grew. I found my old report cards and read with fascination the comments each teacher had written with perfect penmanship.

Walking back through my life again in this way, I realized I was smiling. Tears were welling up in my eyes. I remembered love: the people who had loved me and the people I loved. I remembered the hurt, too: the people who'd hurt me, the people I had hurt. But I loved every moment, every page. I could see there in words and pictures what had always mattered to me. I started to realize how important it is to document for ourselves where we have been.

That experience with the baby books and scrapbooks touched me and prepared me for my eventual enthusiasm for journaling. But I didn't start writing at that point. It wasn't until 1990, when I was beginning my work with women business owners, that I started writing daily, religiously.

Why? Because at the time I thought it was the only outlet available to me. I had made this crazy decision to create something new—and in doing so, I had unknowingly put myself into a position where I felt totally alone. I had fears and misgivings. There were highs and lows to come, and, no doubt, lots of mistakes to work through. Who was I going to talk to? Who was going to want to hear that I didn't always know what to do next?

So, one night, when I was really upset, I just sat down and started writing. Whatever came out. A real stream of thoughts. Some of them made sense. Lots of them didn't at the time.

It felt good, and I began to do it more often. I started to look forward to that quiet time each night. Sometimes I simply recorded the facts of the day. Sometimes I was really inspired and went on for pages. Asking myself questions, pouring out my feelings.

I was starting to get the hang of it, but I can assure you, I wasn't walking around proclaiming the virtues of journaling, not yet. That came several years later.

One night, sitting at home, trying to write in my journal, I realized that I just didn't feel like writing. So I started reading, instead, leafing back through what I'd written in past days . . . and kept reading until I came across an entry I had written two years before consisting of just two short sentences:

> What if we could get 100,000 women to give us $100? That would fix our loan problem.

I stopped cold and just stared at those two sentences. Only a few days before, the *Wall Street Journal* had announced the creation of the

Capital Rose Perpetual Fund: We were going to ask four million women and men to contribute $10 apiece and raise $40 million in order to finance economically viable women-owned businesses. It was the same idea!

I didn't remember—and still don't—actually writing that entry in my journal. I can't even recall what made me write it at the time. I am absolutely convinced, however, that had I not written the idea down when it first came to me, there's a good chance that I never would have acted on it two years later.

Seeing that entry, I was definitely hooked on journaling. And I still am.

Writing gives concrete expression to what's on your mind and in your heart. It's a way to pull together and make sense out of the raw output of your brain, the stuff that doesn't always come out in a straight line or in logical sequence. It's a storage mechanism, a sorting-out mechanism. Our thoughts are resources, and we can use them only if we cherish them and preserve them. Knowing where you want to go has a lot to do with knowing where you have been and how you have felt.

If you currently keep a journal, then you know what I mean, and I don't have to convince you of how valuable a part of this process journaling is going to be. If you used to keep a journal and gave it up, I want you to start again, at least over the course of this journey. And if you've never kept a journal before, then I invite you to begin to communicate with yourself in a new way.

Take the information, the feelings, the thoughts and beliefs that are inside you, and put them on paper, and I believe that with time you will discover there the answers to your questions. Because the answers are inside you, waiting to come out. The trick is capturing them, and saving them until you figure out which answers go with which questions.

There, I've said my piece. The rest is up to you. But remember: There's no pressure here, just possibilities.

The Scavenger Hunt

Now we're going to set up a series of pages in your journal, one each for several categories of information you're going to collect. We're not going to do all the work in each category right now, so leave plenty of space (perhaps a few pages for each category) to write in later as you make new observations.

At the top of one page in your journal, write, "Things people are always kidding me about." First think back, as far back as you can remember. What are those things? Even things you don't do anymore or that are otherwise no longer true of you. Put them all down on this page. And what do people kid you about now? Write that down too, and in the days and weeks to come, listen carefully to the kidding you receive, and jot down what you hear. Serious things. Frivolous things. Things you laugh about and things that make you cry inside.

For now, just keep building your list, and we'll return to do the work later on: believe it or not, we're going to use this list to explore your skills. I know that sounds kind of crazy! But there *is* truth in jest, and in this way we're going to find some hidden truths for you to work with.

Next, I want you to make a similar list, but this time entitle one page in your journal "Things people are always criticizing me about." Leave lots of space for later, and keep adding to this list as we go along. It doesn't matter if you think the criticism is valid or not. Include it all.

Now, there are four more lists I want you to make:

1. What magazines do you subscribe to or read regularly that have nothing to do with your current occupation? If you're a businessperson, forget *Forbes* and *BusinessWeek*. You read those because you think you have to. What matters here are those you read because you want to, especially if they are publications like *Birders World* or *Kitemaking*!

2. Do the same for the books you've read over the last eighteen months. If you read a lot, take as many pages as you need. We're building a portrait of you with these lists, and we want all the details. The guidelines are the same as with the magazines: What is it that you read, fiction and nonfiction, that has nothing to do with earning a living?

3. Now, go to wherever it is that you tack up reminders and bits of paper that you come across and want to keep in sight. I collect mine in the kitchen, right on the refrigerator. Make a list of what's there on your fridge or your bulletin board: schedules, sayings, quotes, to-do lists, grocery lists, whatever. Write it *all* down in your journal.

4. Now I'm going to get you to do something you've been meaning to do for a long time, but keep putting off: you're going to read and organize all those clippings that have piled up in every nook and cranny of the house. (See, you're already seeing some concrete results from this process!) Go ahead, gather them all together, fish them out from the backs of drawers and those shoe boxes in the closet. Blow off the dust, sort through them, and jot down a couple of key words in your journal describing each one. Include *everything:* a quote that caught your eye, an article on negotiating, a recipe for flourless cake. . . . Nothing is too silly or too "trivial." It's all important to constructing this scrapbook of your life.

Okay, enough writing for now. After all those lists, I'm sure your writing hand is pretty tired, so put down your journal and your pen, and we'll turn to another one of the tools you're going to use on your inward journey: your imagination.

Visions Hold Power

AS YOU ENTER POSITIONS OF TRUST AND POWER, DREAM A LITTLE BEFORE YOU THINK.
—TONI MORRISON

Before you do *anything* important, remember to dream a little: see yourself doing what you want to do, see yourself doing it well, see yourself being the person you want to call "me." On this journey, I want you to use your imagination to see it all beforehand.

I know you may already be saying, "Hey, I recognize what she's doing. This is that imaging stuff! Ugh! Not for me. I don't think so."

Yes, for some reason the notion of "imaging" seems to turn a lot of us off. But in many ways, we're all natural "imagers." We rehearse scenes in our heads all the time; we just don't usually label that as imaging. We can all attest to nights where we've tossed and turned and gone over a hundred times what the next day was going to bring: making a big presentation, meeting someone we haven't seen in a while, doing something that we know is going to be hard. In fact, by the time the actual event comes, it can almost seem like déjà vu.

We *have* been there before. In our minds.

No matter what we do, this mental preparation, this imagining it all beforehand in as real a way as we can, is primary to high achievement. Great athletes do it all the time, and you can't call them mere dreamers! They work hard to reach peak performance levels, so if the practice of imaging didn't yield results, they wouldn't waste their time with it.

And they do *spend time* on it. Jack Nicklaus has given a marvelous description of exactly what goes through his mind as he prepares for every shot:

> I never hit the shot, not even in practice, without having a very sharp, in-focus picture of it in my head. It's like a color movie. First I "see" the ball where I want it to finish, nice and white and sitting up high on the bright green grass. Then the scene

> quickly changes and I "see" the ball going there—its path, its trajectory and shape, even its behavior on landing. Then there is a sort of fade-out and the next scene shows me making the kind of swing that will turn the previous images into reality.

The level of detail and texture and *reality* that Nicklaus puts into the mental preview of every shot is astounding. Why does he bother to make it so real in his mind? Why doesn't he just say to himself, "I want to hit a good shot here," and swing? I haven't asked him, but my guess is that doing it the detailed way is what makes it work.

After all, at high levels of achievement, the game is 90 percent mental. And we're not just talking sports, either: the same is true in business, in life: 90 percent mental, at the *minimum*. There are many, many other people I could cite who attest that imagining the success they want to achieve *in detail* is a big part of what helps put them ahead of the crowd.

The whole area of mental imaging has gotten a bum rap, as "flakey" and kind of "soft." But that's selling the process short, considering all the testimony that's available. Unfortunately, the fact that large numbers of us dismiss the idea out of hand prevents more of us from developing this skill, and an important skill it is.

Yes, I said "skill." That's exactly what it is.

It's a skill that's difficult to master, too, much more so than the people who put it down might think. It takes a lot of practice to get the experience to feel *real,* and that's the point at which you get the best results. When you're getting that sensation of déjà vu as you actually *do* the thing you've previously imaged, the door to high achievement is wide open.

So we're going to work on mental imaging throughout this process. Our goal is to have you become so adept at this that it becomes second nature to you.

Let's start right now with something that I'm sure you've already spent a lot of time thinking about: what it would be like to be a business owner. Let's see if we can strengthen the image you have in your mind and begin to turn it into something that's going to drive you forward and energize you.

"But I've already done that a thousand times!" you may be saying. Perhaps so. But much of the time when we "imagine" something, we aren't really imagining at all. Instead, we make suggestions to ourselves, usually verbally: "Boy, it's going to be great when I have my own business! Can't wait until there's no boss to answer to. I'm going to make more money than I ever did before. Maybe I can get that house I've been wanting to buy. . . ." And so on: ideas, sometimes accompanied by fleeting pictures, but not usually very well developed ones.

This time, I want you to just sit still for a few minutes and imagine as deeply and as richly as you can. You've been thinking about a specific business, haven't you?

Now see yourself as a successful business owner. How are you spending your day? Imagine everything: your success, how you and those around you are fitting into the picture, what it has taken to get to this point . . .

Really get into it. Develop the picture. Go further: hear sounds, smell odors, feel yourself move through a full-blown movie of what being in business is going to be like. Then ever further into three-dimensional reality. Keep trying to make it *so* real that it's as if it were in the past instead of the future.

Take as much time as you need with this. If you feel silly, remember Jack Nicklaus and all those tournaments he's won. If it feels like it's not working, if a voice inside you keeps saying, "I can't do this," then stop for a while. Go back to it later, in a couple of hours or even tomorrow. Try doing it whenever you have a free moment. And each time, write in your journal whatever you saw and otherwise sensed and how you felt.

Remember, this is a skill. Like any skill, you are not going to master it overnight. But you can develop this skill—and others—if you just give yourself some room to do it wrong a couple of times. Have a little patience, and decide that you *can* do the things you think you cannot do.

Right now, all you *need* to do is make a commitment to yourself that you *will* develop this skill. Recognizing the importance of developing it is half the battle: do that, and you're already making progress on the road to new achievements.

What If . . . ?

About once a year, I sit down for a couple of hours and go through another kind of exercise. First, I write down twenty-five things I would do if I won the lottery. Or, I should say, I *try* to write down twenty-five things: even though I have many interests, tons of places that I imagine I'd like to go to and things I'd like to try out, when I sit down and give serious thought to what I *really* want to do, I can never reach twenty-five. I don't think that that's because I lack imagination; I think it means that, out of all the things I can imagine doing, only certain options are really in tune with who I am.

Next, I rethink that list by making another one. I try to write down the twenty-five things I would do if I found out tomorrow that I only had one year left to live. Again, I always come up short of twenty-five—and that tells me even more about what's *truly* important to me.

As you can well imagine, these end up being two very different lists. For one thing, the list of things I absolutely must do before I die is always shorter than the if-I-won-the-lottery list. And it's this shorter list that's most important to me: those are the imperatives. Those are the things I want to make sure I'm working on *right now,* one way or another.

I think that it's important for each one of us to know what's on that list. That's the list that should map the direction of our lives. It's a summary of what our values are, what our beliefs are, what really matters to us, who really matters to us, and the actions we are prepared to take. It's a reflection of our spirit. It's the thing that grounds us. It's a yardstick for measuring our actual accomplishments against what we want to accomplish before we die. Long before it.

I know that this yearly exercise of mine may sound like idle daydreaming, but I don't think it is. It may be daydreaming, but it is anything but idle.

For one thing, I (like you, I'm sure) tend to get caught up in everyday living, caught in the rut created by everything I *have* to do. Nothing extraordinary, just the little things required in everyday living.

I'm often amazed at how much time it does take just to live. Food shopping, clothes shopping, dry cleaner's, house cleaning, maintenance, writing a card to a friend, taking it to the post office, gathering with the family, and on and on and on. Finding time to do something as simple as reading a book, taking a bubble bath, or just sitting still for a while seems to require major planning. With all the time-saving devices we have nowadays for our homes, it's a mystery to me where all this time I've been saving has gone!

So I put together those lists first because doing it makes me stop—Stop!—even if only for a short period of time. Second, it helps me enormously in sorting through all the things going on in my life. It gives me a perspective. And it's a good way of keeping myself posted as to what's been going on "in there" while I've been concentrating on day-to-day affairs. I am determined to live a life that matters, and I don't want to wait for a dramatic change in my life, to face loss of health or a loved one, for me to get the perspective that makes me start living the life I want.

So I'd like to ask you to put together your own versions of those two lists. One right after the other, because putting them together at the same time adds a dimension that is missing when you do only one. Take your journal, and on two facing pages write:

- ▲ Things I Would Do If I Won the Lottery
- ▲ Things I Would Do If I Had Only One Year to Live

The first time you do this exercise, write down things that pop into your head. You need a starting point, so don't think too hard about it. Write down, freely, your top-of-mind thoughts.

After you have completed your two lists, copy them down on index cards, and put them in something you always carry with you: your purse, briefcase, wallet, or pocket calendar. Over the next couple of weeks, pull out and look at those lists, compare them, reflect on them.

See if the items on them have staying power. Keep reminding yourself that these two lists are a reflection of what you want your life to be, and give some thought to each item. My guess is that, after you've lived with them for a while, you may want to change some of them, or even take them off the list completely.

Now, after you've spent a little time thinking about these two lists, start to make a third in your journal:

- Things I *Will* Do Before I Die

Next to each entry on this list, write a couple of sentences as to why that one's a must.

> *If I had to choose my driving force, it would be passion.*
>
> Anita Roddick, O.B.E.
> Founder and Chief Executive of
> The Body Shop International

We are going to return to these three lists, so keep working with them. Use the first two to develop that third list of things you are committed to doing before you die. That's the list we're going to use later on in the process to help you determine the right life choice for you.

As your third list develops, I want you to consider what someone very close to you would say if you revealed it. Would the reaction be surprise? Or the comment "That's you, all right"?

A woman who put her lists together with my help showed her third list to her husband. You know what he said? "I can't believe you wrote this! This was not written by the woman I married!" The conversation that followed was life-changing, I can assure you. What do you think your experience would be?

Eleanor, Rod, and Me

WHETHER YOU THINK YOU CAN OR YOU CAN'T, YOU'RE RIGHT.

—HENRY FORD

Lots of "soft stuff" so far, right? Well, I hope you're starting to have a little fun with it, and even beginning to see the point. It's a point that you can really get only by doing, so I certainly hope you haven't just read through this chapter without doing the exercises! If you have or if you've done the exercises but are still wondering whether they have any worth, maybe a story will help explain why I think these kinds of experiences can be so valuable.

A few years ago, I participated in a management training program held in Stone Mountain, Georgia. There were about forty of us executives there for a whole week, and I know that each one of us was harboring thoughts (without saying so, of course) that this was a waste of time. We all had "real work" piling up back at the office.

On the afternoon of the third day, the facilitator announced that we were going to spend some time drawing. I can't remember her words exactly, because, like everyone else in the room, the word "draw" sent me into a mega-panic. I don't think most of us had even *said* the word much in thirty years, much less tried to do it!

Drawing is the sort of thing most of us, at an early age, learn that we cannot do. Remember elementary-school art class? "All right, everybody, we're going to take the next twenty minutes to draw a horse, and then we're going to show everybody our drawings!" I get this sinking feeling in my stomach just talking about it, even now.

But here we were, a bunch of six-figure executives pretending that everything was just fine because in essence we had no choice. It's amazing what someone can make you do if that someone is your employer. No, we were going to draw, *had* to draw, had to choke down those feelings of fear and no-can-do.

Well, no one said we had to like it! That's how I felt, and I was quite sure everyone else was feeling the same. All you had to do was scan the room: the grimaces, the groans, the jokes told the whole story.

The facilitator introduced the woman who was going to teach us how to draw. After receiving a less-than-gracious welcome, she began her presentation.

"Most of us think we can't draw," she said. "The reason is, no one ever taught us to draw."

I liked this woman immediately. She understood how we were feeling. And she was right: No one really *had* taken the time to show us how. They just told us to draw a horse, and then handed back the grade of C.

She started with six or seven very simple rules and techniques of drawing. She explained basic shapes. She gave us some relative measurements: for instance, she pointed out to us that the eyes are a third of the way down the face, not in the middle, where most beginners tend to put them.

Then, after no more than twenty or twenty-five minutes of instruction, she handed out some photographs of famous people and asked each of us to pick one. I picked Rod Stewart. Then she asked us to draw a portrait as close to the original picture as possible.

Well! We looked at one another as though she'd asked us to solve the debt crisis in the remaining half hour.

But as we started, the most interesting thing happened. With the information that she'd given us, I found that I was actually *able to draw.* Not drawing like with those horses in fourth grade, either. I mean really drawing! My portrait really looked like Rod Stewart!

That was one of the best half hours I have spent in many years. Seriously.

At the end of the session, all the participants stood up and showed their portraits, and everyone else's drawing was really quite good, too. In fact, no one wanted to stop! There was that much of a high in the room from learning this new thing. We had all just leapt over a mental barrier that had been set up inside us for years. We went from being a bunch of people who "can't" to being people who said, "Yes I can if you will teach me."

I took my drawing home and, after showing it to all my friends, tucked it inside Jansen's *History of Art*, right along with all the other great works. I was proud of it. I am proud of it. I'd done something I absolutely did not think I could do.

That day, I learned that if I allow myself to try things I think I cannot do, to be touched, even to be put in an uncomfortable position, I can grow in skill and spirit. I learned that I have the ability to do *anything* if someone will teach me. And I learned that an expert can provide me useful information, but it's only when I do something with that information in a way uniquely my own that I can discover places, talents, abilities inside of me that I might long ago have dismissed as beyond my reach or interest. What an experience that was!

For years, my favorite quote has been "You must do the thing you think you cannot do" by Eleanor Roosevelt. I always thought I understood what she was saying, and I guess I did . . . sort of.

But my unsolicited encounter with drawing helped me add new depth to my understanding of what Eleanor was trying to say to all of us. It's not just a matter of pushing myself to do the things I think I can't do. Often, it's a matter of doing the things that I don't necessarily think I need to or even want to do.

For learning to take place, we all need to put ourselves into situations that feel uncomfortable, situations where we feel overwhelmed, where we feel like this might be a tad more than we can handle. Supposed limitations to our abilities are seldom what's really holding us back; it's our fear that limits us. Learning is a process of unlearning—unlearning that fear, first of all.

It's also a process that requires information. The only reason those of us in that seminar room thought we couldn't draw was the lack of training we'd experienced. It wasn't that I couldn't do it, after all! It was that I was never shown how.

All the exercises here—the journaling, the lists, and the various other things I'll be asking you to do—are designed so you will achieve the same things: gathering information and finding inspiration, and learning about yourself. So, the next time you're confronted with something you think you cannot do or may not want to do (here or anywhere), remember Eleanor and Rod!

Into the Woods

You know the expression "to be in the woods"? That's how we often feel when we're trying to make a big decision. Most of us are pretty good at collecting *outside* information, but it's almost always hard for any of us to get a handle on what's happening *inside*. The path in there isn't so well marked.

There's nothing wrong with feeling like you are in the woods, especially right now, with the decision you're trying to make. Not only is there nothing wrong with it, I think it's the mark of a healthy person to admit, "I don't know what I really want to do." It's a sign of inner strength, and I think that the struggle it usually takes to say it proves that you are really alive. I think it's the kind of declaration that can mean that you *are* going to have a life that matters.

There's a well-known naturalist named Ernest Thompson Seton who's remembered in bird-watching circles and beyond for inventing (or at least formalizing) what's become known as the "Seton Watch." There are three steps to the Seton Watch:

1. Go into the woods and choose a quiet spot.
2. Sit down, and keep very, very still.
3. Now open your eyes and *see*.

It's probably one of the most sensible things I've ever heard. You don't go looking for the birds and the other forest creatures. You don't even try to find them, and you certainly don't scurry around chasing them. You just sit. Because doing anything else just doesn't work. To see things as they are, sometimes you just have to sit quietly and be.

When bird-watching, it turns out that doing nothing is the best means of seeing things as they are. In our own lives, though, we reach the same kind of vision through activity, which is the reason for the exercises.

Think of this process as one of setting up a kind of Seton Watch over yourself. Once you've done each activity, completed an exercise, just sit for a while and keep your eyes open.

You may feel as though you're in the woods now. Don't worry. It's a great opportunity.

> Don't keep forever on the public road, going only where others have gone. Leave the beaten track occasionally and dive into the woods. You will be certain to find something you have never seen before. Of course, it will be a little thing, but do not ignore it. Follow it up, explore all around it; one discovery will lead to another, and before you know it you will have something worth thinking about.
>
> —Alexander Graham Bell

3

Do It Yourself; Don't Do It Alone

MY FRIENDS ARE MY ESTATE.
—EMILY DICKINSON

WHEN WAS THE last time someone said to you, "I believe in you"? If your experience is like most people's, it's probably been a long time; it's something we generally hear infrequently, at best.

Maybe *no one* has ever said that to you. My guess is that you may not say it very often to others, either. Yet I am convinced that "I believe in you" are the four most powerful words available to us for unleashing one another's potential. It's really *the* most empowering thing one can say to another human being.

"I believe in you." God! that is a wonderful thing to hear. I love the way it sounds. I love how it makes me feel—and I know how it will make you feel when *you* hear it. I know what it can do for you.

At a very low point in my career, when my self-esteem was at an all-time low, I was sitting at my desk, looking out the window, wondering how I'd gotten to that point. I was literally in the process of asking myself whether or not I was going to make it when my secretary knocked on the door. I will never forget looking up to see her holding out a beautiful flower arrangement. The card read simply, "We believe in you!"

There was no signature, but I knew who sent the flowers: the women professionals I had worked with so closely over the previous three years in developing this new business that I was worrying so much about that day. I was blessed to have a whole "I believe in you" group in my life, and I felt all the strength they were giving me as I held that card in my hand. I am where I am today because of them and for them.

To succeed beyond our wildest imagination, I am convinced that each one of us must find someone who will be our "I believe in you" person. This is a must. I don't care if you're a business owner, an executive, an employee, a mom, a student, or a person in transition from one role to another: if you do nothing else in preparing for whatever change lies ahead, *find this person,* no matter what it takes or how long it takes. It's that important.

For some of us, identifying a person who cares about our success and happiness and who believes in us so much that they can say so isn't a difficult issue. Usually, it's someone who is close to us: a good friend, family, perhaps, even the person we love and who loves us best.

That doesn't necessarily mean there aren't going to be other issues that need resolving. At this point in the process, I'd say that the *main* issue is this: getting that person to understand *exactly what you need from him or her.* You may already have an easily identifiable "I believe in you" person in your life, but you may not be getting the *kind* of support you need.

It's often because this person doesn't even *know* what kind of support we need. It's important, then, for you first to ask *yourself* what you need. You'll be able to openly express your real needs only when you know exactly what they are. Then you will be able to meaningfully, helpfully communicate what you truly want, and that's the only way you're going to get it.

What *is* support, for you? I'd like you to take some time with your journal, and try to answer that question in a very detailed, concrete fashion.

For you, support may mean having this person be prepared to just listen and do nothing else when the time comes. It may mean actually helping you out in dealing with some problem. It may mean being available for 2:00 A.M. phone calls, if necessary. You should be able to define it precisely, in the same way you should be able to describe your market and the competition before going into business. The best way to *help* this person to support you is to be clear about what you need. Leaving it up to someone else to define will inevitably leave *you* disappointed.

The catch, of course, is that you must invest time to give as well as to receive. To *have* an "I believe in you" person, you must *be* an "I believe in you" person. It works only when it's mutual, so the best person to select is someone you can believe in and offer support to as well. There is a saying to the effect of "Whatever it is that you want, give it away and it will come back to you a hundredfold."

Sometimes the choice of an "I believe in you person" *isn't* so obvious. You might be surprised at the sort of people who can fill that role. I've had women tell me that their "I believe in you" person is a neighbor, a minister, a mentor, a friend from years past who they suddenly decided to get in touch with again, or even their accountant or lawyer.

A friend of mine was recently interviewing the managing partner of a large public accounting firm that specializes in start-up businesses. My friend asked the partner what the most important thing was that his firm does for these companies and their owners. His response? "Hold their hands."

Pretty revealing, don't you think? He knew *exactly* what his clients really needed. He wasn't belittling them, either. He was seriously acknowledging that, in this tough situation of being new business owners, they needed the reassurance of knowing that they weren't alone. They needed to have him show that he believed they were going to make it.

Don't think that this is just something to help you get out of the starting gate, either. I have noticed that just about everyone I've met who is highly successful has her or his "I believe in you" person. These successful people have confirmed my observation without hesitation: it has been a key ingredient to their being able to work at the peak of their potential.

On the other hand, I *have* met some people who've achieved great success without an "I believe in you" person, and what I've invariably found is that they desperately *needed* one. A case in point: I recently had a breakfast meeting with the CEO of a new company, an incredibly impressive woman who had both a doctoral degree in science and an excellent track record in business. As you can imagine, she's a very busy woman, so we were just going to have a quick, get-acquainted breakfast while I told her about Capital Rose.

Well, something about the Capital Rose philosophy obviously struck a chord with her, because she talked for nearly an hour about her own situation, outlining all the pressures that came with her position—and she said that she wasn't sure she could keep going.

Why was she telling me, a stranger, all of this? Because, as she said, "I don't have anyone else to talk to."

> *Be optimistic: expect the best from yourself and others . . . no matter what.*
>
> Gail Blanke, Senior Vice President
>
> Avon Products, Inc.

And that was one of the major reasons she wasn't sure she could keep going, despite all of her accomplishments, despite the fact that she'd reached the top in her field. She wasn't the first person I've met who has said so, either; I could tell you plenty of stories. In fact, I've become increasingly convinced that the *more* successful you are, the more you need an "I believe in you" person. It *is* lonely at the top.

Feelings of loneliness can attack you no matter what position you find yourself in unless you have that "I believe in you" person in your life. I've seen so many people struggle to get by without one and have seen the toll it takes on them.

I've also seen—and experienced—how positive it is to have this person on your side, not just as a defense against loneliness, but as a definite asset.

When your "I believe in you" person gives you feedback, for instance, it means something very different from when anyone else does. Lots of people give you feedback: people in your business, colleagues, customers, advisors, friends, family, even perfect strangers. Often, it's invaluable; sometimes it's way off the mark. Sometimes you barely hear it, you're so preoccupied.

But your "I believe in you" person is someone you trust implicitly and completely, someone you know is speaking from the heart as well as the head; what they say sticks with you. Positive comments motivate you to do even better. Constructive criticism is a real wake-up call. You end up thinking about it for months because you trust the source, because you have a relationship with that person—who has your best interests in mind—based on deep mutual respect and commitment.

Make It Real

Now I'd like you to mark your entry into this journey: I want you to "make it real" by calling up your "I believe in you" person and announcing what you're up to. Tell this person that you are in the process of making a big decision about your life, maybe the biggest. Enlist this person as an ally in your quest, announcing what you're going to need for support.

If you start out hesitatingly, that's okay. If you don't have all the details yet, if you can't say just where this journey is going to lead you, if you know only that you're headed *somewhere,* blame it on this book and its crazy author! She won't *let* you decide where you're going yet!

There was one woman who was going through the same process you are, but through our seminars. She called a good friend to tell her she was going to determine, once and for all, whether or not she was going to start a business. Her friend replied, "Thank God! You've been talking about it for seven years now!" You'd be surprised how often that happens.

So, even if this person already knows that you've been considering business ownership, go ahead and make the call or appointment to meet. Make it official. Mark the fact for yourself that there is something different, something unique going on this time. You have set yourself on course to explore, to make a decision, and to act on it.

Tell what you are planning to do, what you have been thinking about, how you are feeling, why you're reading this book. Listen carefully to the response offered.

But, mostly, listen to *yourself.* Hear yourself making the commitment. Telling someone else is the first step in making it all *real.*

Go ahead. Make your announcement. I'll be waiting.

NOW FIND A quiet place where you can be alone with your journal. Give yourself thirty minutes of uninterrupted time. Close your eyes and replay the conversation in your mind.

How are you feeling, now that you have committed to your journey? Because that's what you have just done: taken the first step, out in the world, towards a life that you can call your own. Open your journal and record the conversation. Write down how you are feeling, what you are thinking, at this very moment. Write down whatever pops into your mind.

It's not important how much you write. The only rules for this exercise are that you make the call and that you give yourself the full thirty minutes to think about it.

Learn Something New, Every Day

When I was doing the research that led up to the founding of the intrapreneurial company I told you about in the introduction, my then partner and I decided that one of the best things we could do to prepare for this new venture was to get ourselves "out of the box." We'd been working in one way, in one kind of environment, for a long time. We needed to expand our horizons in order to kick our imaginations into gear and fire our enthusiasm.

One of the best things we did, I found, was to begin to seek out conversations with people who were as far outside our world as we could think of. I started talking at length to people like jazz musicians and painters, grandmothers I met in florist shops, librarians . . . people whose lives had very little to do with the kind of business I was in, people I wasn't even meeting (much less talking to) six months before because I was so busy. And, of course, later on—when I'd identified the market for this new company—I started talking to women business owners.

I was giving an outlet to all of my natural curiosity about people after having spent too much time shut up in the corporate complex, and it was an amazing experience. I found myself listening in a whole new way. I was curious to talk to people for my own reasons, but I'd decided that I just wanted to listen to people for their own sake. I was doing a kind of research, even with the jazz musicians, but I wasn't going in with a set list of questions. All I did was initiate conversations and see where they'd take me. And they took me to fascinating places.

This is something I've kept up ever since. I do it with the women business owners I work with and speak to on behalf of Capital Rose, but I also try to make sure that I keep my eyes open for other opportunities, no matter how busy I am.

For instance, I have had the most amazing conversations on public transportation. Whenever I get on a train or a plane, I make a point of looking for a seat next to the most interesting-seeming people I can find. Sometimes they don't want to talk. If they do, though, I just ask them where they're headed, what they do, and see what they say. I've found that if you're sincerely interested in how people occupy themselves and how they feel about it, they're usually glad to tell you.

I've met some really admirable people on all these trains and planes: a senator; more successful, motivated businesspeople than I can count; retirees full of wonderful stories from *their* years in the trenches; students whose enthusiasm and knowledge absolutely floored me. Listening to them, I always try to discern what makes them tick, why they're doing what they're doing, what they want out of their lives. Most of the people I meet are striving to achieve something, and a very large number of them have met with success; of course, as you can well imagine, I'm also trying to figure out what it is that's made them successful.

I don't ask directly, though. I find that I get a much better sense of the keys to an individual's success simply by listening to his or her story—noticing which parts of it bring a light to the eyes and a ring to the voice and which parts are stated with quiet conviction. And I can honestly say that I think I've learned more about personal success on trains and planes than from all the business books sitting on my shelves at home.

Those lessons had a lot to do with what I've put into this book. Everything I have to offer you here comes out of my own face-to-face encounters with people: my business partners, our clients and all the other thousands of women business owners and prospective business owners I've met, my own "I believe in you" person, and, yes, strangers I've met on the Amtrak Metroliner.

I'm telling you all this because I want you to take advantage of the same opportunity: the opportunity that lies right outside your door, in the form of other people. I've asked you to pick an "I believe in you" person; in a little while, I'll ask you to gather together a specific group of women who will also accompany you on your journey. But I also want you to seek out people on your own and make this active search a continuing part of this process.

I can't tell you exactly who to seek, nor would I want to. Certainly, if you're thinking of going into a particular kind of business, you should be meeting as many people as you can who are already in it, finding out what it's been like for them. I think you'll find that most people love to share their knowledge. But don't stop there, by all means.

So my exercise for you in this respect is simply this: Go out and explore the world. See what you can discover in other people and what you can discover about yourself in the process.

Don't say, if you're tempted to, "Oh, Rebecca, what a lovely idea," and not take it seriously. I am entirely serious. I can't quantify or even outline the results for you beforehand, but your curiosity about other people's lives *will* bring results in your own. Start today, keep it up tomorrow and every day afterward, and you'll see what I mean.

The Chain Fax

The next thing you're going to do is collect some top-of-mind feedback from three of your closest friends and three people you do business with. We're going to use the fax machine because it's so immediate: it can deliver first impressions, which is what you want here. If there's anyone among the six people on your list who doesn't have a fax machine, you can use the regular mail—but make sure everyone follows the rules!

Put together a short note like the one provided here. Be very specific: You don't want them to spend any more than *five minutes* answering your questions. (So don't worry that you'll be disturbing them; you're asking them for their opinions, their valued input, something most people appreciate being asked for.) This exercise works well precisely *because* it gives your respondents very little time to think about their answers. Consequently, you tend to get straightforward, uncensored feedback: their first thoughts, which, for these questions, can be their best, most useful thoughts.

I've done this exercise myself, and so have a lot of the women I've worked with, and we've gotten some very interesting, often surprising, invariably thought-provoking responses. For instance, you know that I'm a business executive. That's what I know, that's what I know I'm good at. Well, in response to question 1, I had friends and colleagues tell me that they saw me becoming (a) a veterinarian, (b) a housewife, and (c) a Supreme Court justice. Now, there was some food for thought!

Our friends and colleagues see different, often bigger talents in us than we are often prone to see in ourselves. They see us from an angle and in a context that it's almost impossible for us to get a handle on by ourselves. We are acutely conscious of our failings; we know our hidden fears. This baggage we carry around undermines our courage. But if someone says something like "You know, you've got so many new ideas about computer programming, I can really see you as the next Bill Gates!" . . . well, it can be magic.

I think the most efficient way to do this exercise is to call first and make sure that the individuals you've selected are available. Then fax them, wait five minutes, and presto! the input starts rolling in.

Important Fax Transmission!

To: ______________

From: ______________

Please take *five minutes*, no more, to answer the following questions:

1. If I had the opportunity to step out of my current role or career and try something completely new, what would you see me doing, and why?
2. If you were describing me to your mother, what is the first word you would use?
3. What are two things you wish I would change about myself? (Be honest, now!) Please, only one sentence for each of the two changes.
4. What do you see as my driving force? In other words, what do you think makes me tick?

I'm looking at some new options in my life, and I would appreciate your candid feedback. And thanks. You don't know yet how much this means to me.

Once you've received all six responses, find some quiet time to think them over. Lay them out on the floor or a table, so you can see them all together.

What are the similarities? What are the differences? Are there surprises, or do you see pretty much what you expected? Do you agree or disagree with each response? Do any of the answers upset you? Why?

Take out your notebook. Using one left-hand page for each question—copy each question down at the top of its page—list the six people and their answers to that question.

The right-hand pages are for you. Take five minutes to record your own top-of-mind reactions to these responses. "He's nuts!" "I never thought about it that way, but I think that's probably right." "I cannot imagine how she got that idea!" "This ticks me off." Whatever you're feeling at the moment.

We All Need Mirrors

One of the things we women do best, in terms of lending other people our support and guidance, is what I call "holding up the mirror." Not just holding up the mirror to show others who and where they are right now, either, but holding up a mirror to their dreams and showing them what they *can be.* We've done it for centuries, for each other, for men, for our children, and we're pretty darn good at it.

For many of us, getting together and simply talking is such a vital experience because it *validates* us. It takes away that feeling that we are in this alone. There have been countless times when I've heard women say, after spending some time together, "Gee, I just never realized that there were so many other women like me. Other people *do* feel the way I feel!"

I believe women have good instincts that lead us to seek out that liberating experience. I call it instinct; it may be acculturation. What we call it doesn't matter. I only know that one of the things I like best about working with other women is that we are, by and large, information gatherers, opinion gatherers. We reach out and ask, "What do *you* think?" And we're generally not afraid to receive feedback, especially from each other.

Holding up the mirror to each other in this way is such a pleasure and so valuable because it's *creative*. It doesn't just reflect, like an ordinary mirror. It doesn't duplicate what is or what went before. It is not more of the same. It creates something new, something better, because we cannot really discover ourselves, especially new things about ourselves, alone.

In that spirit, I'm now going to ask you to form a group of women—women you don't know, or at least don't know well—into what we might call a "mirror circle." I'm not asking you to do it because I think it's a charming idea. I'm asking you to do it because it's a tool to be used, because you'll get from it things you can't get any other way.

The women in this circle are going to contribute greatly to your ability to reach the right decision. As you reveal yourself and lay out your plans for the future, they're going to hold up the mirror; sometimes they're going to reflect back things you don't necessarily want to see, but should. They'll give you that reality check. They'll be able to be both sympathetic *and* objective because they won't be directly involved in the consequences of your decision, and they won't have a prior history with you.

Some or all of the women you choose for your circle may be trying to make the same decision that you are. If so, then that's all to the good. If you can't or don't choose to form a circle composed entirely of prospective business owners, then that's okay too. As long as each of you is in the midst of trying to reach *some* important decision, trying to effect an important change in her life, then you'll be able to work together successfully.

This isn't just about business, anyway, because your decision isn't just about business. The circle isn't a business seminar, and I doubt it could turn into one. I've noticed again and again how, when women get together in a situation that allows for it, conversations that begin on business quickly move to include other topics. We *know* there's no separation between business and the rest of our lives, and we *act* on that knowledge by sharing the "other" facets of our lives, by listening to and understanding how all the elements interrelate. That's admirable, from my point of view, and it's going to be an important part of the process for you here.

Certainly, don't think of these women as so many new cards for your Rolodex. Use this forum to begin taking a very expansive view of how your associations and friendships can help you in your decision and, eventually, in your business. It might be best, actually, to think of your circle as being somehow set apart from immediately practical concerns.

Think of the *time* you spend with this group as set apart, for gathering data and reflecting on it through the mirror of these other women. And realize that, as with any process that takes time, the progress made won't always be evident. It's almost impossible to reach the *right* decision overnight, so be patient with yourself and each other.

Each of you is going to react differently at different points in the life of the circle. Sometimes you'll think it's great to be there, sometimes you'll think it's a waste of time. But I swear, the time you think is being wasted you'll eventually look back on and regard as useful. You'll see how it all added up to show you the way.

"Let's Have Lunch"

Now it's time to be *really* daring, to do a little pioneering in unmapped territory. I want you to call up five women you don't know and invite them to lunch.

Be thoughtful about your choices. You probably *don't* want all these women to be "like you." If you're a businesswoman, don't be so sure that a woman who isn't one doesn't have something to offer; you might want to include a student, a retiree, a homeworker. We never know what we might learn from people, whether about business or about life. In fact, you should even *try* to surprise yourself with your choices, because you should be inviting every opportunity *to see things in a new way.*

So, if you perceive admirable qualities in someone, call her. That's what counts, that these women be women you've admired, for whatever reason. Women you'd like to get to know, women you've heard of or read about. Businesswomen or not, women who own their own businesses or don't. Not "superwomen," but individuals, each dealing as well as she can with her own real-life situation.

Such women shouldn't be very hard to find because they're *everywhere.* They're running their businesses in your town or city. They're sitting next to you in your church, walking next to you in the grocery store. Think of it this way: If you were considering buying a new BMW, then you'd start noticing every BMW on the road, because all of a sudden that would be what's important to you. Once you've decided that finding women who might help you in making your decision is important to you, then you'll begin to notice them all over the place.

On the phone, tell each woman you call that you'd like to talk about her work, her business, or whatever it is that caused you to think of her and that there will be a few others there when you meet. Tell her about the decision you're going to make and that you think she can help you with it. If she doesn't see how, tell her why; you should have some idea as to how she can, or you shouldn't be calling her.

And don't worry, people *love* to be approached as experts. They love to help, and most people love to meet new people, especially those who are obviously passionate about something, which you're going to be.

When you sit down to lunch, suggest that each of you tell the others about herself, in turn: who you are, something about your background, what you do for a living. Start things off yourself. It's a safe situation, after all. You may never meet these women again, or you just might find some real friends.

You'll probably use the whole lunch hour just telling each other about yourselves and asking questions about what you're hearing. In fact, I can almost guarantee that you'll have reached dessert by the time you've gone around the table. I'd also bet that, after dessert, you'll be saying to each other, "We have to do this again, this was so much fun. It was just great to hear about what you're doing, and I'd like to hear more. In fact, this was so *therapeutic.* I don't get enough chances to meet interesting women."

If you haven't already, sometime before that dessert tell them about the circle you want to form, how it's really about mirroring and making any kind of decision. Suggest why each of them, from what you've just heard, might be interested in joining. I'm pretty certain that the idea is going to be novel enough and interesting enough that you'll draw in at least one of them and very possibly more. If you need to, you and the others who agree to join the circle can have other lunches until you have a total of, say, a half-dozen women participating.

No, there's no reason to do it alone, but it takes *work* to make sure that you don't. Start that work right now with this exercise. And, by the way, this *is* a practical test of sorts. If you can't make these cold calls, you're going to run into real problems when it comes to promoting a business. So see how good you are on the phone, at first meetings, at taking the organizing, leadership position. And simply by saying "Let's have lunch" you'll be on your way to finding a wealth of support, understanding, and food for thought.

I met a woman business owner in Connecticut who'd already done something similar to what I'm asking you to do. Even though her group was formed before we'd ever heard of each other, it's a perfect illustration of what this lunch group of yours can be, so I'd like to tell you about it.

She and a *score* or so of other women (a self-selected group, not all of whom knew each other, but all of whom shared an interest in trying this out) simply decided they'd have lunch once a month, sometimes with an agenda, sometimes without one. They meet to talk, in a comfortable yet businesslike setting, about the issues that are important to them as women, as business owners, as citizens, as human beings. That's all, although sometimes they have a speaker. I know because I had the honor of being asked to join them once.

I found that there was a very open feeling to their group. It's not forced in any particular direction, other than the one they decide at any moment they want to go in. It's ad hoc. It doesn't carry the baggage of either support groups or networking. It doesn't have a name, which is a signal, I think, that it doesn't have to go on forever, that these women don't take themselves so "seriously" that their next step will be printing up membership cards and becoming a sort of Rotary Club. They're letting it go where it will, and they're "learning by doing." Those are all very smart aspects to their undertaking, notions you might keep in mind of how *you* might do it comfortably.

I do have some "rules" and guidelines to suggest, though, for when the circle gets established. They're the kind of rules that will help the circle to remain open, flexible, and responsive to each member's needs:

1. *Everything discussed is confidential and belongs to the circle as a whole.* To be trusted you must be trustworthy.

2. *No individual should dominate the discussion.* But there will be times when each of you takes the lead. Each person's concerns are important and interesting, but not so much so that they negate the issues important to the others attending. Remember: You're forming this circle for the benefit of everyone in it, not just for yourself.

3. *No interruptions when someone else is speaking.* One reason women enjoy talking among themselves is that they get interrupted less often than when men are present. That may sound trivial, but the simple ability to get through a sentence can be tremendously empowering.

4. *Give each other the gift of your self-confidence.* Set up a fine of a dollar (toward the tip, say) for every time someone qualifies her statements with "This probably isn't important, but . . ." or "Maybe I'm the only slow one here, but . . ." or other self-defeating phrases.

5. *No arguing.* An opinion is just that: an opinion. We find new ways of looking at the world because we *don't* all agree, but in order to get the benefits, we need to value al-

ternative visions. Discussing things with passion is a great way of sharing. Arguing sets the blinkers on more firmly.

6. *Above all, be honest.* You are not really being a friend if you don't. Feedback is often hard to accept, but practice makes perfect: receiving it in this trusting environment is going to help each of you to get better at receiving it—and taking advantage of it—elsewhere.

This may all sound a bit mysterious. It's a little difficult to explain because, even though I'm going to have specific suggestions as to what your circle might do at various points, where it eventually goes will be determined by the women in it. I can only indicate here its basic function and purpose, which is to be a forum for listening, offering support, and providing feedback. You and the others are going to shape the process to your own ends, and that's very much the point. You're going to learn what it's for by seeing what you can make it become.

So put the book down now, and please don't pick it up again until you've made your list, made those calls, and experienced what I think will prove to be the best lunch date you've had in a long time.

4

My Mother's Story

ANYONE WHO IS GOOD AT ANYTHING IS DIFFERENT.

—OSCAR WILDE

I GREW UP IN a very traditional family. My dad was the breadwinner. That made him the boss and king of the castle. He was usually traveling for the company during the week, though, so our entire life revolved around our mother.

I would have told anyone who asked, "My mom doesn't work." My mom was just that: a "mom." She stayed home and took care of Dan Jr., Tom, Brian, and me. She did everything for us children, and she called us her "most prized assets."

She was a mother's mother, too. Even with three boys, she somehow managed to keep everything looking immaculate, and when I say my mother did it, I mean she did it all. She didn't give us daily chores. She felt that we were going to have plenty of time to work; while we were still kids, she was going to let us be kids, which meant that she spent hours and hours, day in, day out, working hard to have the house always spit-and-polish clean.

I don't know if your mother did this, but at least once a week, mine would move the refrigerator out from the wall and vacuum behind it.

Today, I find that absolutely amazing. My refrigerator hasn't budged since the day we moved in, seven years ago! I can still remember my mom rocking that refrigerator from side to side, as if she could do anything. I thought that she was the greatest.

Coming home from school each day was a treat. One of my most treasured memories is of walking in the door and being surrounded by the smell of cooking. Dinner almost always consisted of meat, potatoes, and a vegetable. My dad grew up during the tail-end of the Depression, and having meat every night meant you were doing all right.

If Dad was out of town, we had a bit more freedom. We didn't have to have a "balanced" meal, so the four of us kids would gang up and convince my mother to make a pizza or submarine sandwiches.

Each night, Mom literally fell into bed after all the hard work she'd done. By the young age of twenty-five she had had four children, and from the day the first of us was born she truly gave her life to us. Every day was spent making our lives comfortable and meaningful.

Each morning, we would thank her by calling the local radio station and asking them to play her favorite Burl Ives song. We would bring the radio into her bedroom and put it next to her ear, and she would wake up smiling, with her four most prized assets right by her side.

Everything seemed just fine. Our mom was always there, always at our beck and call, ready to do anything to make us happy, to fulfill all our needs.

Then my mom started to get older. So did we. One by one, we went off to college, and she was living as a very young empty-nester. That's what happens when you marry at eighteen and start a family right away.

When my mother turned fifty, two things happened. First, she started to go through menopause. Her hormones were completely out of whack: she knew it, and so did everyone else. And she started to say really strange things. Things like "If I had it to do all over again, I wouldn't have had all of you kids!"

Can you imagine our shock? Our perfect mother, starting to question how she had spent the last thirty years of her life. Our perfect mother, saying she wished she didn't have all of these kids! "Mom, which ones wouldn't you have had?" I asked, almost afraid of the answer.

Mom was in limbo, directionless. I had seen her this way before—usually when Dad's company made us go someplace none of us wanted to move to—but always, within a short period of time, she'd come out of it and get back to being Good Old Mom. But this time was different. She wasn't coming out of it. In fact, it was getting worse.

She felt that her life had been wasted, used up for no particular purpose. We kids were all off becoming responsible adults, and Mom just wasn't a big part of that experience. We didn't need her every day as we once had. We weren't even old enough yet to understand what she'd done for us, and consequently had no ability to express our appreciation.

What was she going to do with her life, now that her kids were gone? She remained in limbo like that for what seemed like a very long time.

Being the only daughter, I was my mom's confidante. When I talked to her on the phone, typically once a week in those days, she broke my heart with her pain. I felt so inadequate because I wanted so much to help her, but I just didn't have a clue as to how.

She was looking for something else to throw herself into, something she could devote her life to. But when you've spent your life being "just a mom," you feel very limited in your options. You feel like you can't do anything, like you have no skills, and according to the rest of the world, you don't! When you tell a prospective employer that you've spent the last twenty-five years raising your children, get ready for rejection. About the best most such women manage is to find a minimum-wage job at a fast-food restaurant or retail shop.

I worked with one mother who wanted to start her own business. By the time we met, she had already tasted quite enough rejection. She was fairly bitter about the whole thing, and she summed up the frustration of countless devoted mothers. "I want to be my own boss," she said. "I have spent twenty-five years taking care of my family. I am now worth $5.50 per hour in the job market, after twenty-five years of responsibility. I am worth this much because I stayed home to raise my children. I hate it. If you are a homemaker, you are worthless. But I know I can do something. I have worked very hard all my life."

On Mother's Day you will often year, "Oh, her job is the hardest job in the world." But nobody really believes that taking care of children is any big deal. If we did, we'd treat mothers looking for a second career, after their first one has been successfully completed, in a much different way than we do.

My own mother had worked outside the home before: nothing like a career, just part-time jobs to earn a little extra money and get out of the house once in a while. Her *career* was being a mom; she hadn't prepared for her eventual retirement. So, during our weekly calls, she almost pleaded with me to help her figure out what she was going to do with the rest of her life.

It was so sad. Her pain was so real. I couldn't see any fairness in it. You devote your life to your kids, and your reward is a crushing blow to your self-esteem.

I'm not suggesting that my mother is stupid, either. Quite to the contrary. I thought she was very intelligent, and still do. We'd always said she had lots of common sense. She was a clear thinker; not a college graduate, but a good thinker. I've always thought that she could have been a high-powered career woman if she'd lived in a different time.

But she hadn't, and this just seemed to me to be her sad lot—because the truth is, I couldn't think of one thing my mother could do, either. She was a mother, and that's about all I could see. I didn't think she had any skills. For heaven's sake, she couldn't even type! She just couldn't *do* anything but mothering: cleaning, cooking, and nurturing others. Other than her becoming a retail salesperson, I myself thought my mother was doomed to forced idleness and unhappiness.

Eventually, she decided to do what many women do who are faced with this predicament: She went to school to get her real estate license. "Whew!" I thought, "at least that will keep her busy for a while."

She had absolutely no confidence in her ability to pass the real estate exam. After all, she told me, she hadn't been to school in over thirty years! Somehow, though, she did pass; I say "somehow" not out of my own surprise but as a reflection of hers. It was an important turning point in her life because what my mother did after passing that exam surprised everyone, perhaps herself most of all.

Very quickly, my mother discovered that selling real estate was not her great, newfound love. In fact, she hated it. But she did see a niche that she thought she could fill: for a property rental agency in the Atlanta market.

Most real estate agents are truly only interested in sales because that's where the big commissions are. They look at rentals and see crumbs. My mom saw, instead, a lucrative niche that no one else wanted to step into.

So she set up a business that deals exclusively with rentals. She acts as a rental agent for residential and investment properties and does much more than just rent them: she manages them, taking care of all the upkeep and handling all the finances.

I could scarcely imagine it. My mother, owning her own business. It was just incredible! I am more proud of my mother and the business she has created than I will ever be able to articulate or express in words.

She knows I feel that way. The business represents self-fulfillment, self-reliance, self-worth. It represents to both of us, after years of being the two "girls," the "weaker sex" (and after her being "just a mom"), one success that we both share in. My mom's success said that we do matter, that all women matter.

My mom loves her business and the work she does in it. She threatens to keep doing it until she's ninety, and if I know my mother, she's not kidding. She will probably end up in the Guinness Book as one of the oldest living business owners in recorded history. Now that she has discovered what she can do, it will be hard for anyone to stop her.

I remember the first time I actually realized what my mom had accomplished. My brother was visiting me, and he was showing me a computerized billing system that he had developed for Mom's business.

Looking at some of the printouts, I asked him where he got the numbers I was seeing. They were so big, I assumed they were dummy numbers. He looked at me, smiled, and said, "Those are real numbers, Sis. Our mother has quite a business going."

I was totally blown away. "She certainly does," I thought. My mother was earning more than do 99 percent of all working women—*all* women, including college-educated women, including all those women who had begun to question the wisdom of staying home to raise kids.

I beamed. My mother was out of limbo. She was a bona fide business owner, successful in her own right. My mother, that fifty-something "just a mom" who didn't have any skills! She was in charge now. She was a boss. God love her.

I'll never forget the first time my mother bought me lunch. This may sound weird, but until she started her business, my mother had never done that. For years, Dad bought lunch. Then, once I was out in the working world, I bought lunch. She'd never been able to pick up a check because she never had any of her own money.

I remember we ate in an Italian restaurant. I remember my surprise when, at the end of the meal, she asked for the bill. I remember the look of satisfaction on her face as she took out her new MasterCard corporate card and handed it to the waiter.

My mom was happier than I had seen her in years. She glowed with a sense of independence and self-worth that every woman needs to experience. There is something about making your own money and having control over your life that cannot be duplicated. Knowing that you can take care of yourself, no matter what happens, is so important that it should be a right.

I was so happy my mother had experienced the feeling that comes when you know that you can do it, that you can rely on yourself. Having your mother buy you lunch may not sound like much, but I'll tell you, it was pretty close to everything for us that day. It's one of my most precious memories.

My Favorite Story

It requires a very unusual mind to make an analysis of the obvious.

—Alfred North Whitehead

I have told this story probably a thousand times over the last few years. People are constantly coming up to me and saying, "I heard you speak. I love the story about your mother."

So do I. Not simply because it's about my mother, but because it's a story about so many women. We all know someone who has been through a similar experience.

In a way, it's also a story about *all* women, because it illustrates that each of us has skills and talents that are uniquely our own, no matter what we have done with our lives. Sometimes we have to look very hard to find them and appreciate them, but I am absolutely convinced that they are there in each of us.

Do you know why I think my mother has been so successful? Do you know what skill I think my mother has used to build her business? She likes to talk on the telephone . . . endlessly! That's it: My mother just loves to talk to people, anytime, anywhere, and she *loves* to talk on the phone.

She repeatedly embarrassed me as a kid because she was always talking to some stranger. If we were in the supermarket, she would strike up a conversation with someone in one of the aisles. It seemed like she talked to everyone she saw. I can remember my dad and brothers kidding my mother about talking too much. Me too. Everyone kidded her. She didn't care. She just kept talking.

Well, no one is kidding her now. She's built her successful business around her ability to talk, and to convey over the phone her genuine interest in the concerns of the person on the other end of the line. That was *her* special gift, as funny as that sounds.

Think about it. My mother manages property for owners who are often living in a distant state, even on the other side of the world. The only link they have to their investment is through her—and there she is, more than willing to spend a half hour talking with them, assuring them that everything is okay and that their property is in good hands. She's just amazingly good at creating goodwill and a sense of trust over the telephone, and hers would be a very difficult business to grow if she wasn't.

And what about all that cleaning she did over the years? Well, my mother doesn't move refrigerators anymore, but she has brought to her business the same close attention to making things look nice that she practiced for years as a homemaker. She has a knack for spending money on the right things, and every property she manages looks like a million bucks.

My mother learned what she needed to know to run her business by *living her life*. Without anyone—not even her—suspecting it, everything she did up to the point of starting her business prepared her for success. She combined and leveraged special skills—a couple of traits that nobody, and I mean nobody, would have called skills—to build her business and create something that is a true reflection of who she is.

And after all, isn't that what owning a business should be all about?

I have seen so many times—including when I took a close look at my mother's experience—that it is in our differences, our uniqueness, that we can find hidden clues about the work we will love to do. Our differences *are* our competitive advantage. They are what make us each special as human beings. They are what give each of us the ability to do something that no one else can do.

If you're taller or shorter than most people, you are probably going to be the butt of some jokes about your height. If you dress differently, you'll hear remarks. If you are of a different nationality than most of the people around you, you may have to listen to some particularly unfunny jokes. If you have chosen a different path, you are probably going to endure some kidding, even some downright critical comments.

Most people don't mean any harm by their jokes or even their criticisms (although some do), but this is exactly why we usually spend most of our lives trying to minimize our differences, trying to fit in.

Consequently, those differences tend to get pushed way down and for the most part ignored, which is very, very unfortunate.

Let's go back now to your journal and the lists you made earlier, of things people have kidded you about and things they've criticized you for. I'm going to ask you to look at them now with a new set of eyes. I want you to see your differences, those things people have kidded or criticized you about, as revealing potential skills and hidden assets. And as you look at your lists, I want to share with you another story, to illustrate exactly what I am talking about.

I did this exercise with one of the most talented business owners I know. She has owned her own business for over twenty years and been incredibly successful. When you are around her, you can just feel this air of success.

I asked her to make a list of the things people have kidded her about. She thought about it overnight, and we met the next day to review her list. Here is what she came up with:

- ▲ Being Polish
- ▲ My collection of quirky lamps
- ▲ My use of silly puns
- ▲ My short attention span
- ▲ Being short

As she handed me the list, she said, "I really thought about this a lot last night. Putting this list together really made me angry!" I asked her why. "Because I realized that I could have made a *fortune* on each thing people kid me about if I just hadn't listened to them."

We talked for a long time about her list, about the differences, the unique style that she'd tried to deny in order to fit in, to stop the kidding. It was an epiphany to her because, looking at the list, she could see that it contained tremendous opportunities, including some *lost* opportunities.

About being Polish, she felt that, had she invested more time in refining her language skills and understanding her culture, she could have taken advantage of some global business opportunities that are currently demanding such knowledge. And she almost cried as she told me that, had she continued to collect quirky, unusual lamps, she could have retired by now because their value has skyrocketed so much.

In fact, with each item on her list, now that she was looking at it with a different set of eyes, she saw opportunity. Even in being a punster, being short, having a short attention span, she saw something special reflected, something that could be valuable to her and her business, and she determined to find ways to mine the potential she saw there.

Now I want you to take your lists and do the same thing. Look at them, and think about all the ways that you might turn the things people kid you about and criticize you for into special resources for yourself, your business, your career, your life. You know how it feels to look at the items on those lists as weaknesses. What happens when you see them as strengths?

Write your thoughts in your journal, right next to the lists. "I could have made a lot of money on this . . . I am the perfect person for that . . . I could do that with this . . . I would have been very happy with that," and so on.

> I DIDN'T BELONG AS A KID, AND THAT ALWAYS BOTHERED ME. IF ONLY I'D KNOWN THAT ONE DAY MY DIFFERENCES WOULD BE AN ASSET, THEN MY EARLY LIFE WOULD HAVE BEEN MUCH EASIER.
>
> —BETTE MIDLER

One thing I've found consistently in my work is that an individual's success is usually born and maintained out of no more than a few unique, often very simple and unheralded abilities. As observers, we tend to look at successful people and grant them more attributes than they typically have. But, looking closely, I don't find too many individuals who have it all, who can do it all. There just aren't that many Renaissance types out there.

Instead, the more realistic picture of a successful individual is of someone who sees her uniqueness, who perceives even some very small differences that set her apart from others, and uses them to launch her life. Differences like an unusual ability to develop a relation of trust on the telephone or like being Polish.

I first saw the power of differences, of the things we are kidded about, through the experience with my mother. Since then, I've seen it frequently in the lives of other successful people. That's why it's difficult for me to endorse those lists of characteristics that make for success. Lists encourage you to focus on the accepted norm; they form the basis for much of the kidding. They do nothing but keep our special abilities hidden from us.

> *The happiest and most fulfilled women are those who listen to themselves.*
>
> Maxine Ballen, Executive Director
> The Business Development and Training Center at Great Valley

You find your opportunity looking at and through yourself. It's not out there, it's in here, in you. So, the next time you are the butt of a joke or some kidding, listen intently for the opportunity. Write down the episode in your journal. Think about the differences that give rise to the kidding. If you can't see the opportunity immediately, go back to the incident later, keep mulling it over.

And give those jokers a big kiss. Marcel Proust had it right when he said, "The secret is not in seeking new landscapes, but in having new eyes." Those jokers are offering you new eyes.

Your experiences may not have always been recognized as important, even by you, but they are. Each one of us has what it takes to build a successful life. Each of us has a little something of value upon which to begin building. It's of no significance whatsoever whether or not anyone else sees it. It matters only that you see. At the end of the day, you always meet yourself.

I don't care where you're starting from—whether it's the home, the boardroom, the university, the assembly line, the family-owned business—you have talents and skills that are uniquely yours. You have the ability, working from your experience, to do something that brings you great happiness. I'm not saying that you'll definitely create a business; that would be an empty promise and it's not even necessarily the thing that will make you happy. What I am saying is that you have something to contribute, something waiting to be done that will provide you with the same sense of fulfillment my mom has found. I'm saying that you deserve to find out what that something is.

5

Throw Out Your Résumé!

I THINK SELF-AWARENESS IS PROBABLY THE MOST IMPORTANT THING TOWARDS BEING A CHAMPION.

—BILLIE JEAN KING

WE ARE MORE THAN the sum of our work experience, a lot more. We severely limit our ability to succeed by insisting that you can learn only on the job, that business is just business, that life doesn't teach you anything. That what you do in your life outside of work has no value. We need to put life at the *center,* instead of making it an afterthought, whether or not Corporate America is ready to accept that.

Just look at the traditional résumé. Where does "life" appear on it? On the very last line: "Personal interests—swimming, cooking, and reading." The placement and the imposed brevity of attention paid to all the things that make each one of us an individual are perfectly symbolic of the corporate attitude. But I'm convinced that one line cannot do justice to those activities so relevant to our ability to succeed.

Believe it or not, you *can* learn about business by thinking about swimming, or cooking, or whatever it is that you love to do in your "personal" life because by doing so you learn about yourself, and *that* process is going to teach you how *you* want to and should do business, which you'd never learn at any business school.

I believe your "résumé" should be a complete, detailed picture of your life: your whole life, not just your "career." It should be a statement of your values. It should contain experiences, feelings (yes, I said feelings; aren't they a big part of who you are?), a representation of your entire self and situation. A stranger should be able to read your résumé and feel they *know* you.

If you look up the word *résumé* in the dictionary, you'll find a definition such as "a short account of one's career and qualifications prepared typically by an applicant for a position." The separation between work and the rest of our lives is pretty obvious there, wouldn't you say? Look up *curriculum vitae,* and you'll find pretty much the same definition. But if you consider the original Latin term, you get a sense of what the résumé should be, instead of what it is. The Latin reads as *the course of one's life.*

But the résumé as we know it doesn't show us the true course of someone's life. It doesn't give us the kind of detailed picture that lets us know another person or ourselves.

To find what it is that you should be doing with your life, though, you need to see yourself accurately and completely. The résumé is a marketing tool we use to sell ourselves to others. I want you to put together another kind of document, one that sells you to yourself, because you're doing something much more important than applying for a job: you're applying for a life! You're applying for the opportunity to spend your days *doing what you love.*

So I've spent a long time thinking about an alternative to the résumé. In order to help you to find what it is you love to do and a means to succeed in doing it, I needed to start from scratch. I needed to design something that you could use as a tool for self-exploration, as a map for finding the treasure hidden inside you.

After working with a variety of women who were trying to implement change in their lives—and with the help of successful business owners, psychologists, and human resource specialists, among others—I eventually developed an approach that I like much better than the traditional one. I call what we're now going to create to replace the résumé a *lifescape,* and the art of creating it *lifescaping*.

I like these terms because they put the emphasis where it should be: on life. Any description of who we really are must be centered on life, not work.

Lifescape: It makes me think of a complete, panoramic scene. There's a sense of movement to it, of drama and action—a feeling that, each time you look, you're going to see something new. Instead of showing an assemblage of discrete objects with no relation to one another, it's a picture in which every detail becomes part of a meaningful whole. Oh, there are definitely some details that stand out, but within a context that doesn't lend itself to easy, abstract summary.

> *All the talent, training and experience in the world isn't worth a thing without a little something called Soul.*
>
> Heather Weir, President
>
> AerobiKicks Venture

My lifescape is a truer picture of me, and giving it a new name—thinking about it differently—helps me to create it, see it, internalize it, in a fresh and revealing way. After all, our purpose is discovery and insight, not the same old, same old.

The Six Spheres

In the next section, we're going to spend six chapters creating your lifescape, piece by piece. Each chapter corresponds to one "sphere" or aspect of your life:

- ▲ your personal resources
- ▲ your day-to-day activities
- ▲ your relationships

- your physical being
- your relationship to money
- your key beliefs

Although we'll create your lifescape piece by piece, we'll be doing so only as a matter of convenience. The six spheres are analytical tools, but that's all they are: we're never going to lose sight of the fact that your life is a seamless whole. The whole point of lifescaping, rather than résumé writing, is to show you that these spheres are completely interrelated.

Not just interrelated, in fact, but indivisible. It's when we start *artificially* dividing—divvying up the pieces of our lives and putting them into separate boxes with labels like "work" and "personal"—that we get into trouble. We're going to use our six spheres to break down the barrier between work and life.

As we look at each sphere in turn, mapping your lifescape, seeking to reflect the breadth and depth of your life, I'll ask you to take all the time necessary for you to see each one of these aspects of yourself and your situation with new eyes.

You'll be doing much of the work that's coming up on your own. I want to reiterate, though, that it's vitally important that you not "do it alone." At certain points I'll be suggesting that you turn to your "I believe in you" person and your mirror circle in order to broaden your perspective on a particular exercise or topic as it applies in your life. But, please, don't wait for my cue. Whenever you feel the urge to discuss what you're thinking and feeling with someone else, follow up on it.

At the end of the next six chapters, we're going to put the six parts of your lifescape together, and your completed lifescape will show who you are and where you are, right now. After that, we'll turn to your past, seeking clues there that will help us to home in even more precisely on the elements you'll want to build into your future. Finally, we'll use the concept of the six spheres to form a detailed action plan for creating the life you want to lead: a balanced, integrated life from which all artificial divisions have disappeared.

Out with the Old, in with the New

First, though, go find your résumé. I want you to understand exactly what it is that we're leaving behind: not just your résumé, but the entire résumé mind-set.

Take a few minutes to read it again, word for word. Now, forget about its usual purpose. Aside from its usefulness in getting a job, would you say that it really shows *who you are?*

I think I can answer for you: No. It doesn't even come close.

It's someone *else's* definition of who you are and a pretty lousy one at that, based on the same standards used in the companies we work for: conformity, efficiency, depersonalization. It says nothing about you, other than where you went to school, where you've worked, what titles you were able to talk someone into giving you.

For years, I've worked with executives who were masters at hiding who they are from the rest of the world, to the point where they themselves have no real idea of what they know, what they are good at, what they can do. What they know is their job title, their job description. Ask someone what they *do,* and ten to one the answer will be something like "I am a vice president at XYZ Company." But how do you *do* vice presidenting?

When I started hiring people at the corporations I've worked in, the company would usually provide me with a list of recommended interview questions. Essentially, they wanted me to work my way down the interviewee's résumé, asking very standard, cut-and-dried questions about what I saw there. I tried it for a while, but I found pretty quickly that I wasn't really learning anything about the person sitting across the desk from me. And, after I tossed out the recommended questions, I began to get a reputation as a tough interviewer. Why? Simply because I'd ask things like "How do you spend your day?" I wanted to know what the interviewee could *do.*

A big part of what I call the "résumé mind-set" is knowing only what we are called, not what we can do. We strive for titles—and settle for them—rather than finding out what it is we love to do. We're all prey to this confusion of priorities.

In the same way, the résumé mind-set makes us assume that more is better: the more skills, talents, etc. that we have, the better off we are. We look for quantity rather than depth, mastery, or differentiation. We respect only the "big" talents, those with recognizable labels, like leadership, and try to convince everyone that we possess them.

We load everything we can into our résumés. We have learned to pose, to present ourselves, to sell, package, and camouflage ourselves. Presentation and positioning have triumphed over substance. The emphasis is on selling the external world on what we appear to be, not on knowing and showing who we really are. And no wonder: it's been drummed into our heads that that's the way to get a job. Most of the time it works, too.

> *Never turn away from your gifts. In their expression lies the power to release you.*
>
> Karol M. Wasylyshyn, Ph.D.
> President
> Leadership Development Forum

But the future will be different. Count on it.

I am absolutely convinced that in the not too distant future, you will see the résumé and the whole process associated with it thrown out the window. In the future, to succeed, we are each going to have to understand and use the skills—even the *one* skill—at which we excel so that we create a competitive advantage for ourselves, for the company we own, or for the company we work for. Our corporations need to accept this new way of thinking, too, and help each employee to achieve honest *self*-assessment in this new way, if they're going to build the kinds of effective teams necessary to succeed in tomorrow's business environment. The criteria for evaluating employees are already being redefined as "ability to change," "ability to learn quickly," "ability to cooperate." Can the ability to talk on the telephone be that far behind?

So get ready to say good-bye to your résumé. Not just to the document, either: You're going to say good-bye, symbolically and psychologically, to the whole mind-set that lies behind the résumé. Then we're going to create together something much more useful, much more true, to take its place.

Read your résumé one more time. Say good-bye to this outdated, overmanaged way of looking at yourself. It's constraining. It is in no way a reflection of the *you* that we are looking to describe.

Now tear it up into little pieces.

And burn it.

PART II

Lifescaping

6

The Treasure Hunt: The Resources Lifescape

IT IS NEVER TOO LATE TO BE WHAT YOU COULD HAVE BEEN.

—GEORGE ELIOT

MOST OF US HAVE SKILLS, talent, and potential that we never use. Many of us find a way to use them only later in life.

Think of Winston Churchill. He was one of the greatest leaders in all of history, but was he a "born leader"? For most of his life no one thought so, and Churchill would have probably agreed. But a time came when something made him a leader. Some explain it by saying he was a "situational leader," not a "natural leader." Those are just words to me. A leader is as a leader *does*.

I wonder whether Churchill's capacities mightn't have emerged earlier if he hadn't had a *label* stuck on him that said "not a leader." It's exactly the same problem I complained about earlier, in regard to those lists of "key success traits": just like lists, labels are confining. They start defining our capacities before we've even had a *chance* to discover what it is we can do, because *we act out our labels*.

Tell someone she's not a leader, and she probably won't act like one. Tell someone she can't draw, and she will never pick up a pencil. Examples abound of these self-fulfilling prophecies.

But it's worst of all when we put these self-limiting labels on *ourselves*. Churchill did that: he was often filled with self-doubt. Thank goodness, though, when the crucial moment arrived, he tore off that label that said "not a leader" . . . and he simply started to *lead*.

Harry Truman is another good example of someone who finally refused to be limited. Prior to his presidency, there was hardly a trace of leadership skills evident in his life, hardly a success of *any* kind. In fact, the label most people put on him read "failure." If he'd accepted that label—or bothered with lists of characteristics of a great president, for that matter—he might never even have campaigned! Then, "all of a sudden," like magic or something, he's got the right stuff!

Bull. He had it all along. It's the label that was wrong.

Yes, examples abound of self-fulfilling negative prophecies. But there are also countless examples of people who have suddenly revealed personal resources that no one believed existed, often not even themselves. And there are countless examples of people who *know* they have some characteristic, some skill, some resource they might tap into, but who may take years to discover how; when they do, though, they become unstoppable.

For each of us, locating, unearthing, and using these resources is part of the ongoing process of life. There is no set time frame: it can sometimes take a long while to identify our best resources and determine how we should apply them. The fact that we haven't found something *yet* doesn't mean it can't be found.

And there are no set rules to tell us which of our personal characteristics have the potential to become valuable resources and which don't. It's not at all unusual for people to take a characteristic that society or they themselves thought of as negative, and turn that negative into a positive.

I'd like you to keep all of this in mind as we begin to construct your resources lifescape. Try to suspend any value judgments about which of your personal characteristics are "good" and which are "bad"; and to put aside any feelings of discouragement or guilt that may have accu mulated over the years regarding resources you might not have developed as much as you would have liked to. It's time to make a fresh start with an open mind, a feeling of self-acceptance, and a will to be everything you can be.

Unearthing Your Resources

> I BEGAN TO HAVE AN IDEA OF MY LIFE NOT AS THE SLOW SHAPING OF ACHIEVEMENT TO FIT MY PRECONCEIVED PURPOSE, BUT AS THE GRADUAL DISCOVERY OF A PURPOSE WHICH I DID NOT KNOW.
>
> —JOANNA FIELD

It's often said that people use only a fraction—something like 5 percent—of their potential. Maybe it's true. If it is, then I suppose you have to up it only a couple of percentage points to be a great success! So let's get started on doing what it takes to get you to where you want to be.

The first step in drawing up your resources lifescape is to describe yourself in such a way that you can see where your potential lies. I'd like you to begin by listing your personal characteristics, those things that uniquely define you. I mean *all kinds* of personal characteristics: intellectual, emotional, physical, and general personality traits, as well as any unique gifts or talents you may have. And don't forget to look at the "chain faxes" you got back and in your journal for material like the list of things that people laugh at you about: we want to get all the data we can.

Don't worry, you don't have to get everything down in one sitting. Like many of the exercises you'll be doing, this one becomes more and more fruitful the more you go back to it and refine your responses.

Again, don't be judgmental. Don't censor yourself. Underneath a "bad" trait that you might hesitate to write down there may be *treasure:* a clue to a hidden resource. For instance, I once asked a market researcher what made her good at her job: "I'm a nosy person," she replied. Can't you just see people complaining or making fun of her because of it? But she found a way to apply that character trait and turn it into a valuable asset because she'd looked at herself both honestly and uncritically.

To get you started, I'll give you some examples of the kinds of characteristics the women I've worked with have listed.

Intellectual Traits: good with numbers . . . verbal aptitude . . . linear thinker . . . conceptual thinker . . . enjoy studying and research . . . uninterested in studying . . . think fast on my feet . . . left-brain thinker . . . right-brain thinker . . .

Physical Traits: energetic . . . lethargic . . . need to eat frequent meals . . . don't care when I eat . . . skip meals altogether . . . ambidextrous . . . physically fit . . . out of shape . . . graceful . . . uncoordinated . . . take a lot of naps . . . don't need much sleep . . .

Personality Traits: curious . . . love to work hard . . . peaceful . . . talkative . . . . emotional . . . withholding of affection . . . caring . . . generous . . . stingy . . . nosy . . . hate to get bogged down in details . . . meticulous to a fault . . . sloppy . . . ambitious . . . lazy . . . funny . . . grate on people's nerves . . . shy . . . outgoing . . .

Unique Gifts or Talents: perfect pitch . . . artistic . . . accomplished gardener . . . leadership qualities . . . intuitive . . . good conversationalist . . . good public speaker . . .

As you can see, I've divided the responses into categories, and even paired some of them up, for the sake of illustration. There's no reason, though, for you to do that when you're making your own list. They're all part of the whole you, after all, and what you want to do at this point is simply get them all down on paper as they come to you.

If you can do that more easily by writing in sentences and paragraphs, rather than lists, go right ahead. For instance, Caroline, one of the women I worked with, started out this way:

I'm organized and logical. I deal with things straight on. I work best with projects that have a beginning and an end. I'm compulsive, and can be obsessive. I don't think clearly if I can't get things in order.

I work best with people who are dependable and willing to take responsibility. In my present situation, I work hard at being diplomatic and supportive. I must have a positive attitude; subtlety is not one of my strengths. I feel like a mother to thirty children, and I find it exhausting.

I'm honest and dependable. I work well independently. I like brainstorming with people with similar interests and a common goal, however.

If I feel secure, I can be impulsive and have fun. . . .

As you can see, writing in full sentences and paragraphs helped this woman to develop her thoughts and move from one set of impressions and perceptions to another. If I ask you to do an exercise in a certain way, it's only because I've seen that that way works for most people, but if you want to do things a little differently as we go along, then by all means do so. If you don't get the results you expected from doing it another way, you can always come back and see if the "tried-and-true" method works for you, after all. Whatever works for *you* is what you should do.

So get out your journal, and see what personal characteristics you can think of this time around. And remember, you can always go back and add to the list.

CONTRARY TO WHAT a lot of people would tell you, I simply don't believe that the key to success lies in your ability to acquire skills and knowledge. Developing skills and gaining knowledge is not the problem; it's a given. No, developing the *right* skills and seeking out the *right* knowledge as they relate to you is the problem . . . and the solution.

Think in terms of the "resources" you can perceive in yourself, including those that don't look like "skills" or "knowledge" at all. Skills and knowledge are objective possessions that you can always acquire, one way or another. *Resources,* on the other hand, include skills and knowledge, but they also include all those subjective traits that you just listed.

So, now that you have your list of traits, I want you to start looking at them in a new way: as resources. Understand that, while you may think of particular traits as being "good" or "bad," there are no "positive" or "negative" resources; there are simply resources, any of which might be drawn upon as you build your new life. Thinking of *everything* about you as a potential resource really gets the imagination working.

First of all, *you control* those resources, you control the time and energy you're going to put into their development. As you review your list, some resources will undoubtedly seem more developed than others. Are there ways you might be able to invest time and energy to make an undeveloped resource a greater asset? Such a sense of self-empowerment leads you to seek out further self-knowledge, which *is* the key to success.

Now take a moment with each personal trait and consider it in this new light. As you do, note in your journal any thoughts that arise.

THE SECOND STEP is to make a list of things you *love to do.* This list should also be as exhaustive as you can make it. Look into every aspect of your life, personal and professional, public and private, for those moments that make up the best part of your day. It could be anything, anytime, anywhere. Nothing you love or love to do is too small or insignificant to be included: it could be singing Broadway show tunes or surfing in cyberspace, spending time with your kids or bringing a meeting to consensus, or even just sitting down at your kitchen table and eating cookies. (Remember, Mrs. Fields got started because she loved *baking* cookies.)

As an example for this exercise, I'll show you what Caroline wrote: "I like . . ."

to plan a dinner party
to decorate my home
to write
to talk with friends
to knit and needlepoint
to brainstorm
to go out to eat
people who are creative
everything in its place
to read
to manage money
to teach things to people
going barefoot
to organize things
to share common concerns
to sit by the fire
to know where I'm going
leadership activities
thunderstorms

Her list was full of variety, and yours should be, too. Don't worry about what it all means right now; just pick up your journal again, and get it all down. Take this opportunity to rediscover *you*.

NOW YOU'RE GOING to make a list of the counterparts in your life: things you *dislike*. On a new page, record everything you can think of that you don't like or don't like doing. It could be something you do only once a year, like visiting your grandmother in the nursing home (hey, I said you need to be honest, didn't I?), or much more frequently, like paying the bills. It could be a particular part of your job at work. It could even be something you did only once and will never do again.

Here's what Caroline's list looked like. She wrote: "I don't like . . ."

to clean
to "chat" on the phone
confusion or disorganization
listening to complaints
traffic
to fly
many vegetables
handling telecommunications at work
what gravity is doing to my body
gardening
heights
unfinished projects
to barter
to fire someone
emotional confrontation
computers/technology

Again, don't censor yourself. With all these lists, it's okay to free-associate. Nothing is too insignificant. Nothing should be left out because it's too unpleasant or embarrassing, either.

NOW WE'RE GOING to organize all these lists, and put them into a visual matrix that will give you a clearer idea not just of your resources but of what you want to do with them.

First, take two blank facing pages in your journal and divide them into a grid by drawing a horizontal line across them both, halfway down the page. This gives you four quadrants between the two pages . . .

1	2
3	4

. . . with the following labels:

Quadrant 1: Love to do and do a lot
Quadrant 2: Love to do but don't do as much as I'd like
Quadrant 3: Dislike but have to do
Quadrant 4: Dislike and want to eliminate

Now take those last two lists—things you love and things you dislike—and assign each item to one of the quadrants. Start with the list of things you love: they'll be going into quadrants 1 and 2. The things you dislike will, of course, go into quadrants 3 and 4.

To show just a few of the items that Caroline put into her matrix:

1 **LOVE TO DO AND DO A LOT**	2 **LOVE TO DO BUT DON'T DO AS MUCH AS I'D LIKE**
to read to write to brainstorm to go out to eat be with people who are creative to talk with friends to teach things to people to organize things to share common concerns to know where I'm going leadership activities everything in its place	to plan a dinner party to decorate my home to knit and needlepoint going barefoot thunderstorms to sit by the fire to manage money
3 **DISLIKE BUT HAVE TO DO**	4 **DISLIKE AND WANT TO ELIMINATE**
to clean to fly many vegetables computers/technology handling telecommunications at work	to "chat" on the phone confusion or disorganization listening to complaints traffic gardening what gravity is doing to my body unfinished projects to barter heights to fire someone emotional confrontation

Rotating the Crops

This matrix isn't a mere static picture of your likes and dislikes. It's a *perceptual map, a tool you can use for determining what actions you want and need to take* to create the life you want. We developed this tool for use in our seminars at Capital Rose and found that for a lot of people it really brings to light some ways of initiating positive changes in their lives.

When you diagram your life interests in this way, as opposed to just making a list, you can actually visualize the possibility of movement and change. You can see that it's possible to "rotate the crops." That's what those arrows and that big X are for: by moving items from one quadrant to another, in the direction of the arrows, and by eliminating from your life the things you don't want in it, you begin to take real action towards creating the life of your choosing.

Of course, I'm not talking about just moving words around or taking an eraser to quadrant 4! Your matrix isn't a box on the page: it's a representation of what you're doing with your life, and a source of clues about what you *could* be doing. It can help you decide what sort of business you might want to run. It can reveal ways of taking things you're doing right now for free and turning them into a source of income. It's a marvelous tool for seeing not just what resources you have but also the potential for transformation that lies waiting in them. Let me show you what I mean.

Quadrant 1 is, well, nirvana. It's doing what you love. You definitely want to make more space "in there" for some of the items in quadrant 2. You'll also want to see if there's any way for you to transform some of the items in quadrant 3 into things that you love to do (after all, some of those things in quadrant 3 may be the things you do best).

Quadrant 2 shows you opportunities for positive movement. If it's something you love, then you want it to have a bigger place in your life, right? How can some of these items be developed, moved into quadrant 1? Through expending some combination of time, money, and energy, in most cases. But if they can't be moved, at least be on the lookout for ways to connect the activities here with those in the first quadrant: it can be the key to finding *exactly* the right way for you to end up spending the majority of your time (including all of your working hours) doing what you love.

Let's skip to quadrant 4. This is a great place for finding clues when it comes to arranging your life. For instance, I don't like gardening any more than the woman whose matrix you just looked at, nor am I good at it; therefore, before I buy a home, I need to consider the fact that I might be happier living in a town house so that I won't have a lot of yard work to do. And items in this quadrant that can't be immediately avoided or eliminated can at least be minimized. Where there's a will there's a way, and as you make advances in accentuating the positive, believe me, you are going to find the means to do that.

Unless, of course, one of those items really belongs in quadrant 3—a very tricky quadrant, indeed. Here, you need to carefully analyze each item to determine whether it can be transformed and moved either to quadrant 1 ("Love to do and do a lot") or to quadrant 4 ("Dislike and want to eliminate") . . . and, if so, which way.

For instance, this person hates to clean, but let's assume that she's very good at it. Let's also assume that on her list of resources, there's an item that reads "I can make people laugh." Combine that with "writing" in quadrant 1, and who's to say that this person couldn't make a career out of being Erma-Bombeck-Meets-Hints-from-Heloise? This may be aiming pretty high, but there's no reason to immediately discount that kind of possibility. Aim high! And when you look at your own matrix, above all, look for the connections, especially those you've never thought of before.

Another example: This person doesn't like dealing with telecommunications and other kinds of technology. On the other hand, she does have a knack for organization, leadership, and (over in quadrant 2) managing money. Upon further reflection, she might decide that it's not the technology itself that she dislikes: it's the corporate culture of the stodgy phone companies that provide the service; her own company's tendency to buy into new technologies without thinking through beforehand how they're going to be used; and the unmotivated people in her workplace who allow the situation to go on as it stands. If she has resources in analysis and problem-solving, she may very well show her company how to purchase and employ various telecommunications options more efficiently and inexpensively while at the same time organizing things in such a way that she gets to deal with aspects of telecommunications that she *does* find enjoyable, and to delegate the other aspects to the right members of her team. (See how this process can get results in Corporate America?)

> *The success of a businessperson can be measured by the problems she has successfully solved.*
>
> Betsy Z. Cohen, Chairman
> Jefferson Bank

Notice that, in each example, it wasn't just a matter of looking at "likes" and "dislikes": you also have to figure out how to make the best fit between items in those two categories and items you find on your list of resources. That's the key to achieving meaningful success. If you concentrate only on your resources, you may do well, but there's no guarantee that you're going to end up with a form of success you can live with. And if you don't look carefully at your resources, determining which ones you can bring into play now and which ones need further development . . . well, you may know what you *want* to be doing, but how are you going to get there?

Luckily, the exercises you just did make it difficult *not* to begin to see the connections. When you make very thorough, free-ranging yet precise lists and then analyze each side of the equation in terms of the other, I've found that particular resources invariably attach themselves to things that you love to do. Knowing what you love to do also makes it much simpler to decide which resources are worth developing—by investing time and energy, or even money, possibly in the form of tuition for a course—and which are not.

Other resources may point the way to eliminating or transforming things you dislike, as in the telecommunications example. And they can even provide valuable, often surprising clues as to how to turn some of those "negative traits" into truly positive resources; I'm convinced that, essentially, this is the thought process that that "nosy" market researcher went through.

Sometimes the connections are monumental, sometimes they're very simple. Sometimes they're obvious; sometimes they're subtle and take imagination to perceive and act upon.

> *Expertise and cleverness are important, but you need wisdom to become an effective leader and have a successful life.*
>
> Helen H. Solomons, Ph.D.
> President, Harrison Associates

And sometimes they don't lead to action at all, but to some sort of insight into what makes you tick. I know a woman who runs one of the leading organizational development companies in the country; she's also a mystery fan, has been since she was a little girl. She did this exercise and realized that she loves handling organizational development problems because it's like unlocking a mystery. Understanding this may not directly affect the way she does her work, but it adds to her self-knowledge and will undoubtedly fuel her enthusiasm.

I HAVE ONE LAST exercise for you to do, to put the final touches to your resource lifescape. First, spend some time analyzing the matrix you've created, going back over your lists and your reflections on the ways you've characterized yourself. Make sure that they're the best representations you can achieve of who you are and what you want to do.

Now, turn the page. I want you to do some writing—no more lists for the moment!—to bring these very internal exercises together before we step outside and take a look around, so to speak.

Think about your gifts: those resources you've listed. Are you using them to enhance your ability to do the things that you love? What connections do you see between them and your loves and dislikes? What connections and synergies might you develop in the future?

7

Where Does the Time Go? The Activities Lifescape

I MUST GOVERN THE CLOCK, NOT BE GOVERNED BY IT.
—GOLDA MEIR

I CANNOT REMEMBER the last time I didn't feel guilty about something. It's not the type of guilt that comes when you have really screwed up. No, the kind I live with is that guilty feeling that comes when you can't do all the things that you would like to do or that the people around you would like you to do. There are times when I'm going in every direction at top speed, with the zeal of a missionary—and it seems as though my great reward is to feel guilty as hell that I can't do more. As each day comes and goes, I feel more and more like I want to stop and get off of whatever ride it is I'm on.

I tell myself that it's just a matter of using my time efficiently, concentrating and praying that nothing unexpected occurs to throw me off stride. It's really a matter of prioritizing my day. I know I can do it all. I want to do it all. I love all the individual pieces of my life. The trick is figuring out how to put them all together.

Why do we insist upon doing it all and then on beating ourselves up for falling short of perfection? I think the answer lies in our need to care deeply and to express it. We do make decisions about our own life, our own needs, but those decisions seldom diminish our caring about others. It's not a zero-sum game for us where, in order to get something, I am going to take something away from you. We rarely say, "If I add this, what must I unload or ignore or put on the back burner?" No, we are apt to say, "I want to do this, so I'll have to figure out how to add it to my list, fit it in with all the other things I'm doing."

We are trying to do too much. I really believe that is true. But we are doing too much because we want to, we love to, and—in some ways—we have to, for our own sake.

There was a time when women were focused entirely on the home. Then came a time when many of us decided to try focusing entirely on our careers. Perhaps it's easier to be focused on only one thing, but I don't think we want to accept that way of life any longer, whether it means being focused only on the home or only on a career. Deep down, the positive feelings we get in return for how we have chosen to live our lives far outweigh the guilt we carry with us, at least on most days.

We have a tremendous blessing that life has bestowed on us. We have a great capacity to use our minds and our hearts, which in part make us who we are; and everything good requires some time, some work, some pain. Most women I have talked with wouldn't trade the opportunity to use both their minds and their hearts for anything in the world.

So, what can we do, short of throwing in the towel, becoming one-dimensional, giving up part of what we love? I think there are several things that we can do to keep it all going and to ease the burden of feeling guilty:

1. First, recognize that you cannot do it all well, all of the time. None of us can. There is nothing defective about you. Give yourself permission to not be perfect every day.

2. Ignore those women who want you to believe that they can be an executive vice president for a bank, bake cookies, run the Girl Scout troop, commute two hours to work each day, cook a gourmet dinner every night, entertain regu-

larly, and be the perfect life partner. They are lying through their teeth. They may be able to pull it off once in a while, but not consistently. Leave them to their own fantasy, but don't increase your own guilt by believing them.

3. Don't focus on trying to change the people around you. We have control over *ourselves*. It may not always feel like we do, but we must realize that we are the architects of our days. We do have the ability to say no! That's where we need to focus. I think, in doing that, we have a better chance of a payback.
4. We need to build into our lives the notion that it is more important to do the things that matter most than to try to do everything. Everything may *seem* important, but it's not. Some things are a matter of personal habit; some are traditions; some are just the way it's always happened. Developing the ability to think through and decide which are the really important things that you need to do will help you succeed on all fronts. Other than in sales efforts, quantity alone almost never defines or produces success.
5. Most of the things that eat up your day you have chosen: try to keep *why* you are doing what you are doing top-of-mind. We tend to focus on the to-do's, the have-to's, and we lose sight of the why's. Focusing on the why's provides a perspective and a grounding that the to-do's conceal.

If you work on mastering them, you'll be surprised at the impact these five simple suggestions can have on you and your daily life. To help you do that, try developing a summary of the five points, using just a few words for each, that will jog your memory. I have boiled down the five points in this way, for my own use:

1. Perfection isn't required every day.
2. Forget the fantasy!

3. Be the architect of your day.
4. Do the right things.
5. Why?

While the points may seem to be just plain common sense, they're easier said than done, I can assure you. To really incorporate them into your life takes lots of practice, the way any new skill does. But this skill will help you at the office, at school, at home, and inside you.

Create your own reminder list. Write it down and keep it somewhere convenient so that it will be a constant reminder to you. Put it on an index card and carry it with you, on a Post-it Note attached to your bathroom mirror, or on a big sheet of paper that you can't miss seeing. Hang it where you'll see it everyday at home, at the office, or both.

I have my list hanging on my refrigerator. When I'm preparing dinner each night, I use the time to unwind and slow down. It's some of my best thinking time, so I like to have my list there during it. It reminds me of what I am trying to accomplish. It helps me look at the day I have just put in and determine how I'm doing. It helps me decide what is important for tomorrow.

Now, before we construct your activities lifescape, I'd like you to do some writing in your journal on the subject of time—how you're using it and how you'd like to use it. How does the prospect of spending more time investing in yourself make you feel? Is there a possibility that making an investment in yourself is going to take away from time spent on others? Does that make you uneasy?

Are you currently spending enough time during the week doing things you love to do? Do you think that you *have* enough time in your life to make the changes you've been dreaming about? Let's see.

Your Activities Lifescape

Your activities lifescape shows how you're allocating your time, how you expend your energy, and how the actions that fill your days express what's important to you. In order to understand these things, you'll need to look in detail at the way you've been spending your days. We'll start by using the matrix of loves and dislikes that you constructed in the previous chapter.

First, identify those items on the matrix that you get paid for doing and those you don't. Paid work is just that: your job, your business, whether you do it every day or on the side, or even work you do for barter. Unpaid labor includes any labor you do for someone else: volunteer work, raking leaves and painting fences at your church, watching the neighbor's kids, *and* time you spend taking responsibility for family and family concerns or handling aspects of the household. Unpaid labor also includes time spent on self-development activities.

Mark each set of activities with a different-colored highlighter. How many of the paid activities are in the "love" quadrants, and how many in the "dislike" quadrants?

Look at the unpaid activities in quadrants 1 and 2. In creating your new life, one of your goals will be to get paid for doing (or to run a business in which you get paid for doing) things you love. You want to begin right now to consider the possibilities. At first blush, it may sound like wishful thinking. You're probably saying to yourself, "No one would pay me to do *this!*" Don't be so sure. You are good at what you love to do, you are creative with things that you love, and you can be successful at doing something you love much easier than at something you feel you have to do. *If you can articulate what it is that you love to do, you just might be able to make a living doing it.*

Of course, it isn't possible or necessary to be paid for everything we love to do, but anything in these two quadrants can serve as a clue. For instance, you notice that a lot of your friends seek out your advice; just as important, you enjoy listening to their problems and helping them. Combined with the right resources, loves, and other factors, this could lead toward getting a degree in social work or counseling, writing articles on the subject, or some other way of getting paid for following this interest.

This is just one example, but the possibilities are endless. Spend some time brainstorming in this regard about the items in those two quadrants; refer to your list of resources.

Take this opportunity, also, to see if there is anything you forgot to write down in any of the four quadrants of your matrix. This is something you should do periodically as you continue to advance through the rest of the spheres. Self-discovery is an ongoing process, and things that seem insignificant can, upon analysis, actually become keys to making the right choices.

NOW, WITHOUT CONSULTING your daily calendar or appointment book, estimate how much time you're spending each week on each activity, paid or unpaid, loved or disliked. Write your estimate next to each item.

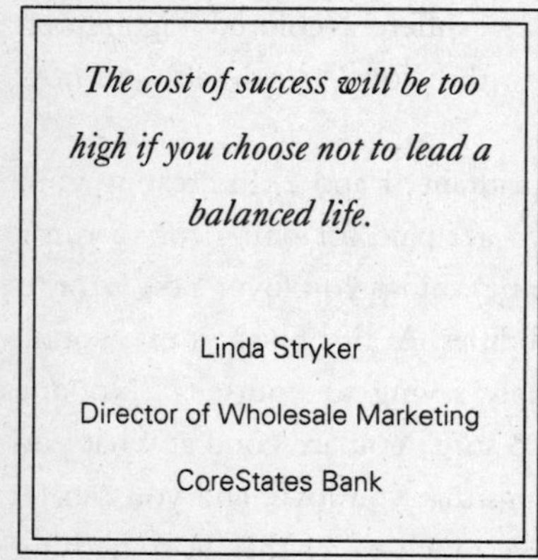

When you're finished, get out your daily calendar, your appointment book, or anything else that will help you to precisely track the hours in the day: notes taped to your refrigerator, a schedule from work, to-do lists, even scraps of paper with appointments scribbled on them. Once again, double-check your matrix to see if you've left anything out of it. Look back over your schedule for at least the last couple of weeks, and write down the actual hours you spent on each activity next to your estimates.

If you don't keep a daily calendar and can't track where the time is going, then the first step of the exercise for you should be to do so for a week or two. Carry a small notebook with you, and write down how you're spending your time. Then go on to the next step.

Why *did* we do this in two steps, first with an estimate and now by referring to the calendar? Because how we spend our days and how we *think* we spend our days are almost always two different things. I've found this to be true for myself and for just about everyone who's done this exercise with me. Tell me whatever you want to about yourself, and I can almost guarantee you that your daily calendar will tell me something different.

You can run (I'll bet you do a lot of that!) but you can't hide. This is your life in that matrix. How much time in your day do you spend investing in yourself, improving yourself, growing as a human being, having fun? Because that's what spending your days doing what you love means.

How much time did you *think* you were spending on things you love? If there's a disparity, one way or another, between your estimates and the reality of your schedule, how does that make you feel? Why do you think you might have estimated incorrectly?

Look at the balance of time you're spending between paid and unpaid work. Look at the distribution of each over the four quadrants. Are you content with this picture? I assume not, or at least not entirely, or you wouldn't be reading this book.

Spend some time writing in your journal on this question. Concentrate on your feelings concerning the ways you're currently spending your time and how you might prefer to spend it. Use the matrix, but also think about any recent incidents in your life that come to mind that relate to the way your time is allocated. Here are some selections from what other people who've done this exercise have written:

> I realize that I'm spending time on volunteer activities that I really don't enjoy doing. They use up a lot of my energy, they're not helping me with my career advancement, but mostly the activities I'm involved in aren't making a difference and don't seem worth the effort.

> I requested a shorter work-week so I could spend more time with my kids, and I took a pay cut. But it turns out that I'm doing the same amount of work—the only difference is that I have to bring the work home now to get it finished! I'm being paid

less, I'm no longer viewed as being on the fast track, and I'm not getting as much time with the kids as I thought I would.

I realize that when I have free time, I'm either scuba diving or thinking or reading about scuba diving. Maybe I should find a way of making a living at it.

I looked over my calendar for the past year and realized that I had cancelled all of my doctor appointments for business reasons. I'm not making myself my most important priority.

I don't really like my job, but one good thing about it is that I can almost always leave right at 5:00. Looking at Quadrant 2 in my matrix, I suddenly realized what an advantage I have: maybe I can find some night school courses that will help me to get a job doing something I love to do.

Diversifying Your Self-Investment Portfolio

Now that you have a clearer notion of how you've been spending your days, I want to go back to one of the ideas I brought up back in chapter 1: the importance of investing in yourself. Specifically, I want to urge you to find ways of investing in yourself that you may not have tried before.

There are several types of investments in yourself that you need to start making if you haven't already. Some you should do daily, like eating well and getting enough sleep (we'll return to the importance of taking care of yourself physically later on). Others are more periodic. Some are big, some are small. They are all important contributors to your success.

Right now, though, I want to concentrate on one particular kind of investment: doing new things. I mean, especially, the sorts of new things that really challenge you—that often mean putting yourself into a situation where you don't feel completely comfortable. Not a dangerous situation, certainly, but an experience that draws on and develops your resources in new ways. This can be a wonderful investment in yourself and invaluable preparation for creating your new life.

For each of us, that challenging experience will be different. For instance, if you were afraid of heights, then making a commitment to spending a few more minutes each day looking out a high window, getting used to the view, could be terrifically liberating. You wouldn't have to run out and go bungee-jumping in order to get returns on that investment: just looking out that window for a minute longer each day will work positive changes in every aspect of your life.

You see, I'm not talking about just racking up new experiences. I'm essentially talking about overcoming fear.

When I was in high school, I was deathly afraid of getting up on the balance beam in gymnastics. Tennis was everything to me, and I convinced myself that I was protecting myself and my ability to play tennis by not getting up there. But I was really just afraid, and besides, I didn't like doing things that I wasn't good at.

I drove the gymnastics teacher *crazy* with my refusal even to try until one day, in utter frustration, she said, "You know, you could improve your tennis dramatically by getting up on that beam and trying it." With all the wisdom of adolescence, I thought she was out to lunch, like just about every other adult I knew.

It was only years later that I realized I had missed a great opportunity to invest in myself. She was trying to tell me that getting outside of the comfort zone is what promotes growth, and it really doesn't matter if there's a connection to what we do every day or not. It's all in the stretching. To this day, I regret not getting up on that balance beam.

You're confronted with opportunities to do new things, difficult things, each and every day. You must already have things in mind that you've wondered about doing, that you've been meaning to try. Well, you've put them off long enough. Look at your list of resources: I *know* there are things out there that you've been thinking of doing that will help you to further develop some resources that aren't fully developed. Or, how about finding a *new* way to spend some time on quadrant 1 of your matrix—especially if it means performing at a higher level of achievement than you've attempted before.

And remember that example of the woman who found a way to change her feelings about dealing with telecommunications? Is there something in your quadrant 3 that could also be transformed into a love if you tried approaching it in a new way?

For example, I have a friend who was always kidded by her friends and family for spending an enormous amount of time "sweating the details" of things. Everything had to be just perfect; so much so, in fact, that people routinely called her "obsessive-compulsive." She really grew to dislike this aspect of herself because she was teased about it all the time. Eventually, however, it proved to be an invaluable trait. She got involved in contract law and has an amazing reputation in the field precisely *because* she is so attentive to all the nitty-gritty details.

> *Living well is a kind of inexact science: the more you experiment and take calculated risks, the better your results.*
>
> Antonia Cottrell Martin
> Founder and President, Foundation for African American Women

Whatever you choose as your new investment, whether it's one thing or a few different things, choose something challenging. Now take your calendar and schedule in some time over the next few weeks for the new, and then use that time as scheduled! You won't regret it.

Oh, and while you've got it out, I'd like you to put one more set of appointments into that calendar of yours. I'd like you to decide which times of the day are best for you when it comes to really concentrating on this process. I'd like you to mark down—in ink!—some time for your journaling, some time for your mirror circle, and some time for us to be together over the days and weeks to come.

Spending time to discover who you are and what your true strengths are is an essential, infinitely rewarding form of investing in yourself. It's also an experience that's undoubtedly going to take you out of the comfort zone. It calls for you to overcome fear, and it's the best way I know for moving forward.

Where Should the Time Go?

Now that you've looked at your calendar as it stands, I want you to construct your *ideal* calendar. How would you like to invest your time and energy? What sort of balance do you want to strike between all the various elements of your life?

Referring to your matrix and your lists of resources, draw up in your journal a weekly schedule the way you'd like it to be. Put in everything: work, play, exercise, time with friends or family, time alone—even include the time it takes to do the laundry or sleep or simply sit in a park and watch the clouds roll by. Fill up all twenty-four hours of each of the seven days.

Now, compare your ideal calendar to your current schedule. What thoughts and feelings come to you as you look at the differences? Record them in your journal.

Finally, do some brainstorming over how you can get from your actual calendar to your ideal calendar. Remember, it's done step by step: How might you move at least *one* entry from quadrant 2 to quadrant 1? How might you take the first step toward being paid for doing what you love to do?

Focus on the small stuff. You've spent your entire life worrying about the big stuff: degrees, jobs, titles. Sweat the details, the things that really make you who you are, now. Look back through your journal, use it in your thinking.

Use your imagination because the answers may not be obvious. Think back to my mother's story. Can you imagine her calendar and her matrix before she started her company? They probably wouldn't have looked anything like those of a future business owner! But buried in all that cleaning and cooking and talking were things my mother was able to combine to create a life that she loves living. Your clues are buried in your lifescape. Sometimes it takes a lot to find them, but they are there.

So, before you go on to the next chapter, try to come up with these clues that will help get you to your new life. Here are some things that others have written:

> I was thinking about the fact that I love to read fiction. Sometimes I feel guilty about taking time to read something that doesn't directly contribute to "building my knowledge base." But I've started to notice that I have a clearer mind and a better perspective after I've read a few chapters of fiction. Maybe it's because I let my brain disengage: I've actually been stuck on a problem, and come back to it after I've read something unrelated, and the solution seems obvious. I never would have thought before that reading novels was a tool for solving business problems.
>
> ———
>
> When I actually figured out how much time, door to door, I spend commuting, I was shocked. I spend fifteen hours a week just getting into the city so that I can spend time on the phone and with a computer. I really need to explore telecommuting options—even if it's only two days a week. I could use that six extra hours once a week to investigate some business opportunities of my own.
>
> ———
>
> I love beer. When I travel, I get excited about trying out local brews I've never experienced. In fact, I've done some dabbling in home brewing, and I really enjoy that as well. There's got to be a business idea in here somewhere. Beer importing, maybe? What about starting a microbrewery? Beer is really starting to become stylish these days, and I've found a lot of women who also really enjoy beer. I think I'll go flip through my home brewing file.
>
> ———
>
> I realize that I don't get to see my extended family as much as I'd like. My grandmother is getting old and I don't see her

nearly as often as I should. She's such an important person to me, and yet I seem to let business get in the way of scheduling time to see her. Even though she never puts pressure on me to get together, I know she's disappointed. I need to make it a priority to take her to lunch, just the two of us. I've just let things slide. I can't continue to do that.

I need to recalibrate my week so that I don't end up spending the whole weekend "vegging" just to get ready for the upcoming week. When I try to fit things in, it feels like a struggle, and I'm not enjoying them. I work so intensely during the week that I end up wanting to just be by myself on the weekends, to recuperate. I *know* that when I schedule time *during* the week to regroup, my life is far more productive in general. Sometimes I forget that, though. I need to be more aware of how I'm spending my time during the week, so that I can have productive and enjoyable weekends, too.

You see that some of these clues relate quite directly to a person's business. Others relate more to quality of life.

We have a long way to go before you'll put together an action plan for the rest of your life; right now, like the women I've quoted above, all you're looking for are clues, perhaps a hypothesis about where the yellow brick road might take you . . . and perhaps a smidgen of courage.

8

Yours, Mine, and Ours: The Relationships Lifescape

WE CANNOT BELIEVE THAT IT IS FIXED IN THE NATURE OF THINGS THAT WOMEN MUST CHOOSE BETWEEN A HOME AND HER WORK, WHEN MEN MAY HAVE BOTH. THERE MUST BE A WAY OUT AND IT IS THE PROBLEM OF OUR GENERATION TO FIND THE WAY.

—1919 SMITH COLLEGE PUBLICATION

IN OUR SOCIETY, women are at the center of life. We are the glue that holds it all together. We are always in demand, always on call, and we try to do it all because it all matters to us. Through our many and varied relationships, we nurture, support, develop, give, love, rear, care for, and sustain those around us. We have been blessed in that.

To protect our blessing, we have been forced to work extra duty as we have made our way into the working world. Our role as "keeper of the home fires" didn't vanish or change as we took on new roles. In fact, *none* of the expectations that defined our lives prior to entering the workforce changed or went away. We didn't want them to.

Women do not neglect their families and children to become successful out of the home. They just work harder and longer and become more focused. For women, it's not a question of one or the other, but of how to put it all together so that it works—for everyone. We seem to be happiest when we are participating in the full circle of life. That's not to say it hasn't proved to be hard as hell.

A business owner recently wrote to me expressing the situation many of us find ourselves in:

> Here I am—running between the computer, trying to get this proposal out, helping Molly do her homework, washing her hair, getting a bedtime story. Am I trying to grow a business or grow a child? Sometimes they work at cross purposes. I love each in a different way. Can I do it all—and be there fully for both?
>
> Damn—I feel like a walking model for your customers, Rebecca—what do we learn from me? How to avoid insanity, love deeply, care deeply, be loved, and be the best I can be in my business? Tune in for the next episode.

In these words, I can feel how important each part of her life is to the woman who wrote them. I can also feel the pain and frustration associated with trying to do it all. Sound vaguely familiar to you? It's a situation that most of us can identify with.

I'll never forget the day when we were having a meeting of the officers of Capital Rose. While discussing one of a hundred urgent matters that were on the agenda, we were signing signature cards for a bank account we were opening. The cards were being passed around the table. When they reached one of my partners, she looked at it and said, "I don't think I can sign this."

She told us she had been up all night crying because she felt she was letting everyone down. Her other business needed her. The board needed her. Her husband needed her. Her daughters needed her. She is the sole guardian of her younger brother, and he needed her. Her friends needed her.

Tears were welling in her eyes. "I'm not sure I can do this," she continued. "I know I can make a contribution to the company, you know how committed I am, but I don't want to shortchange you. I just don't know if I can hold up my part of the responsibilities."

I have talked with countless other women who were in the same situation. Golda Meir summed it up when she said, "At work, you think of the children you have left at home. At home, you think of the work you've left unfinished. Such a struggle is unleashed in yourself. Your heart is rent."

But this was different. This was happening right in my own company, with my partner! It's different when it strikes that close to home. And it's different when the individual it happens to is an incredible, talented woman who always seems to have it all together. She seems like a superwoman. Then, one day, you discover she's not. She's like the rest of us.

"While you guys work on the business—while I *want* to work on the business—I sometimes need to play Mom" is a difficult thing to say, regardless of the environment. Even when it's only women in the room, it's a hard thing to get out on the table. You're going to feel guilty. It's hard not to, especially if you are committed to both.

So after that, we all made some adjustments. We have a flexible work environment. We try to allow ourselves to fit our work into our lives. We rotate our priorities from one day to the next, between the work we all love and the rest of our lives, which we also love (and the importance of which we trust the others to understand). We try to minimize for each other the deeply felt guilt we occasionally give voice to.

But I don't want to kid you, it's not easy. Building a company, having a family, raising kids, are each of them full-time jobs. There are times when we wish she was there and not off doing something with her children. I think she wishes that too, sometimes. But we go forward, and we accomplish a lot, in spite of it all and because of it all.

The Relationships Lifescape

Your relationships reflect who you are as clearly as any other aspect of your life. You are interconnected with other people, and the connections you form with them can influence you profoundly. They speak of what you value and the kind of legacy you want to leave. Like the other lifescapes we have worked on, this one holds a wealth of potential information about what you might want to do with your life.

I believe that our relationships fall into three categories:

1. *Given Relationships*—We didn't choose our parents, our brothers and sisters, our grandparents, our aunts and uncles. (They didn't choose us either, something I know I often forget!)

2. *Chosen Relationships*—We choose our significant others, our husbands, our friends, our associates, our neighbors, or at least the neighborhood. This is a group that we have the ability to *un*choose if we so desire.

3. *Desired Relationships*—These can be just as "real" for us as those that already exist, because we're intent on making them real. Desire for a relationship can be based on love, interest, status, career, loneliness, or curiosity. Sometimes it's planned, sometimes it just happens that we suddenly want a certain relationship. In any case, it's longing from afar.

I'd like you to spend some time now looking at the photos you have of people in your life. Leaf through your photo albums or look at the pictures on your bureau, and think about the relationships you have with the people you see in them. Which were given and which chosen?

Now, make two lists in your journal: of people with whom you have Given Relationships and people with whom you have Chosen Relationships (either personal or professional). Group people together within the categories according to their relation to each other, in reality or as you see them being related. Get everybody in there. If you came across a special photo that has deep significance to you, you might want to place it in your journal as part of the lists.

In a certain sense, your life is depicted in these names and photos. These lists are a mirror in which you can see yourself.

Let's first work with the relationships that you were given. Make two new lists, one on each side of a page: what are the things that you absolutely adore about the people who make up your givens, and what are the things you absolutely cannot stand? These givens can be the best thing that ever happened to you. They can also be terrible. Usually, they're a mixture of both.

Someone I worked with gave me some food for thought after she looked at her lists:

> When I was young, I was incredibly conscious of how different my family was from the rest of the world. Often I was *self*-conscious about it. Now that a lot of them are gone, I realize how much of my own uniqueness has to do with the very unusual environment I lived in as a child. I still remember, however, the feeling of pain that not being like everyone else brings to a child. It's so ironic that as a child I yearned for "normalcy," and now, as an adult, I want nothing in my life so much as to be an individual and to be unique.
>
> I was definitely my father's child—he was affectionate and laughed a lot. He always believed in my ability to do anything. He travelled a lot, though, and I hardly ever saw him. My mom was very cold, and always the one to tell me the things that I couldn't do. She always made me feel bad about who I was and what I wanted in life. She never told me I was pretty or smart or said that she loved me. For years, I blamed my lack of self-esteem on her. Now that she's gone, and I am a parent, I realize that she was the strong one in my parents' relationship, and that she had a very hard life with my dad being on the road all the time. I am much more forgiving now.
>
> I always used to wonder how I would have turned out if I'd had a warm and loving mom. But I realize that *I'm* a warm and loving mom, and I guess that's really worth a lot.

I think that no matter how we've felt about our Given Relationships in the past, there are always new ways of seeing them, and those in turn can provide new ways of looking at ourselves. So go ahead.

NOW THAT YOU have your thoughts on paper, let me ask you this: What would your journal look like if I asked you to go over everything you just wrote about these people and highlight all the things that are true of *you,* too? Which half of the page would have more highlighting on it?

I have a feeling that there are some things here—things about *you*—that you haven't thought about in a long time. Take some time for reflection, and then write about who *you* are in your journal, as seen through your Given Relationships.

NOW LET'S LOOK at the other faces, of the people you've invited to share your life: your Chosen Relationships.

You've honored them. Not everyone is or will be asked to participate in your experience. Who did you ask and why? What was so special about them? What did you need? What promise did you hold for them? Why did they say, "Yes, I'd like to share in your life"?

Don't just answer these questions in your head. Take each person, one at a time, and each question, thinking them through and writing your answers in your journal.

THE LAST THING I would like you to do for now with these three groups of people is to answer the following questions (in your journal, of course):

1. In what ways are my Given Relationships and my Chosen Relationships similar?
2. In what ways are they different?

3. Who are the people in my life who have influenced me the most? How and why?
4. What do these similarities, differences, and influences say about me? What do they reveal about the choices I've made?

You can go beyond those questions, of course. They're just a starting point to lead you to reflect on what your relationships in general mean to you. Here are some excerpts from what other people have written:

> As I look at the relationships in my life, I see more clearly the magnets that attract me to the people I love. I have always been drawn to people that are storytellers. As a child, my life was filled with stories and adventures from around the world that my sea captain father told. My husband is a master storyteller, as are my business partners and my best friend.

> I am drawn to brilliant and energetic people, both in my personal and professional lives—although it sometimes exhausts me to keep up with them. I get afraid, in my low-energy times, that I will become my mom, and lose my zest for life. I realize that many of my chosen relationships are designed to ensure that I will never become my mother, and that I enjoy relationships in which a lot of affection is expressed. I think that our child feels very loved by his parents, and that makes me feel good. I am so aware of expressing my love when I am with him.

> Looking at these names and faces, I realized how much my friendships with my women friends mean to me. I draw inspiration and courage from them, even when they're only in my thoughts. I need them in a completely different way than I need my husband, whom I love deeply. But doing this exercise also

> made me realize how little I get to see these friends, now that I'm a working mother. I don't even have a picture of my best friend that isn't at least twelve years old!

YOU'VE JUST CREATED a lifescape of the people who matter to you . . . with one exception. Remember the third category?

I want you to put together a description of a future relationship, one that you would love to have. It can be a romantic relationship, a friendship, or maybe even a relationship with a business partner. Here's what one woman wrote:

> Even though everyone talks about trust and open communications today, few know what the words really mean. I want to team up with people who are dedicated to the highest quality solutions—without the hidden agendas of self-promotion or turf-building. I want to participate fully, become thoroughly absorbed in the work, and be stimulated by the momentum that a good team can create. That's the kind of exhilarating work relationship I'm looking for in my future.

What are you looking for? Write it down.

When you've finished, take some time to think about what you've just written, and ask yourself why you want this relationship in your life. Why haven't you been able to find it yet? How does that make you feel? Again, write it down.

NOW THINK ABOUT the decision you're trying to make and what it will mean in your life and in the lives of those people on your lists of Given and Chosen Relationships. Try to anticipate whether or not each one of them will be supportive, should you decide to start a business, go back to school, or implement any other kind of major change in your life.

We don't always support the decisions of the people we love, do we? It doesn't necessarily mean we love them any the less; it just means that we can't—or won't—go along with them on this one. Unless you're very lucky, you're probably going to have to deal with at least some resistance, for any number of reasons, from one or more of these people. On the other hand, many of them are going to be strong allies as you head into your new life. And, since people and circumstances are never simple, some of these people are going to resist your decision . . . but end up supporting you in the end!

Take some time to think about the reactions you might expect from each one of these individuals. Try to understand why, too. Consider each person in turn, from the littlest children—even a baby is going to notice and react to changes in the family—to the oldest adults. Write down, next to each name or picture, some notes about what you anticipate from that person. If you have any ideas about how you're going to deal with resistance and encourage support, write them down too. You might even want to go to a new page and consider this question at length.

> *Life is too short to spend it working with people you don't like.*
>
> Christine Patton, Chef (former Senior Managing Director, Manufacturers Hanover)

This would be a very good time for you to consult with your "I believe in you" person. I imagine that this person knows of many of the people you've listed. Her (or his) observations about them can be invaluable; in fact, you may find that you need to rethink your assessments of the reactions you'll be getting after the two of you have talked over your hopes and fears.

Even if your support person doesn't know these people, she knows you. She can help you to explore your expectations and strategize concerning any difficulties that you foresee. Most of all, though, she can simply listen to your concerns.

The members of your mirror circle can help, too, although from a different perspective. In many ways, it's often easier to discuss one's relationships with people who aren't directly involved with them. Of course, you don't have to go into any details you don't want to go into; at the least, however, you can learn how they deal with concerns and situations that may be very similar to yours.

BEFORE I GO ON to talk about some of the problems that building a business can cause in your personal relationships, I want you to add one more picture to the gallery: yours. It's only fair that *you* get to be in your own journal!

This picture is a reminder that the answers are going to come from you. You can ask others to help you stir the pot, but you are the chef.

If you don't have a picture of yourself that you're happy with, have one taken. I think it's important to have a picture of oneself that is flattering. Put a picture in your journal that cries out "You bet, I'm up for this!" Give yourself a boost.

Getting Your House in Order

I can't say it enough: there is no separation between work and the rest of the life of a woman. That's why, when a woman starts to tell me about her great idea for a business, I am very quick to stop her and say, "Don't talk to me about the idea, I want to talk about you. Don't talk to me about the business plan, talk to me about the other people in your life, your most cherished relationships."

Those are the determinants of success, and those are also the derailers. From seeing far too many painful situations, I know that if a woman is worried about getting an accountant before she has taken the time to think through the role her relationships will play in her business, she is heading for a fall.

Whatever your current situation, your new one is very likely going to be more demanding in significant ways, especially if you do start a business. Don't let yourself be lulled into thinking that you'll gain flexibility and freedom that you don't have now. What you're going to gain is the opportunity to squeeze all the same to-do's—and more—into different time slots.

If businesses are established without sufficient consideration given to the business owner's relationships, subsequent failure of those businesses can almost *always* be traced to problems arising from lack of support, unexpected demands, unmet and often unspoken expectations, and personal loss. This is particularly true with husbands, significant others, lovers, or life partners.

If you are seriously considering starting a business or, for that matter, considering any major change, you have probably already discussed with that number one person in your life what it is that you want to do. I take that as a given. What I *don't* take as a given is your understanding of the response you received—and you shouldn't, either.

Do you really understand what is meant by someone saying, "I just want you to know that I am supportive of whatever you decide to do?" Does it mean: "I am going to be there for you. I realize that things will change. We will both have to make some adjustments, and I'm okay with that." Or does it mean: "You have my support as long as you don't lose any money, get home by five, and don't interfere with the way our life is now."

I worked with one woman who got well into the start-up of a retail business—with her husband's support—but when it became obvious to her better half that she was going to have to work most weekends, the support quickly began to fade away. Now, you can say that everyone knows that a retail business involves weekend hours, and this should not have become a problem. You can say they should have known. In the thrill of the start-up, though, you make a lot of dumb assumptions. Ask any business owner.

Reality sets in, for most of us, not in the planning phase, but when something we are used to having isn't there anymore. Being away from home night after night, working long hours, and doing it seven days a week has a way of putting your loved ones' level of support to the test pretty quickly. All of a sudden, you are fighting two battles: one on the home front and one in the business.

I am not suggesting that you should doubt the sincerity of your life partner's enthusiasm and support. I am encouraging you to clarify it, understand it, discuss it, and make sure you are both singing from the same hymn book. Depending on how well you communicate with one another, finding workable solutions to the changes that will occur in your life together can be either manageable or else distressingly complex.

Having built a foundation of understanding and an openness to discuss the changes and the give-ups will help both of you to weather the things you didn't anticipate that will inevitably come up. Without that understanding between the two of you going in, the unplanned events and unforeseen changes can easily kill your business—or, for that matter, whatever new endeavor you're going to head into—and quite possibly your relationship.

In addition, for most of us, communicating with our significant other is only the first step in our preparation. How will your decision affect your children? How will *they* respond to the changes that are lying ahead? How will *you* respond?

One woman told me how she had arranged it so that she could work out of her home. Every day, she would get dressed, say good-bye to her two-year-old son and his baby-sitter, then walk out the front door, around to the side of the house, and into her home office. Her son knew that was where she was going, but she had trained him to understand that when the door to her office was shut, Mommy was at work.

He respected that. He never opened the door. He would just throw his little body against the door, crying, "Mommy, Mommy, no work!"

Another woman business owner related that she told her teenage son, who was very upset that he wasn't getting from his mother all the attention he was used to, "I have a right to be happy, too. I love my business. That doesn't mean I don't love you." It didn't stop her from feeling guilty as hell, though.

Believe me, I'm not suggesting for one minute that personal relationships always get in the way of business success; in fact, they can be your best source of energy and inspiration, and if you're doing what you love, your personal relationships actually become enhanced. I'm saying that it takes a good deal of conscious effort and planning to make sure that they support your efforts and do not become detractors, stumbling blocks. After we have done the work of understanding ourselves, of determining what it is that we as individuals want, the next step is to cast a wider net, one that includes all those people we want in our lives and who are depending on us.

Take one pencil in your hands and try to break it. It breaks easily. Take two pencils together and try to break them in half, and it is much more difficult. Put five pencils together, and they are almost impossible to break.

Our relationships are our strength. Engendering the support and commitment of your loved ones for your new endeavor is your insurance for success. In your new endeavor and in your new life . . . and not necessarily in that order.

AT THIS POINT, you may be leaning toward business ownership, you may be thinking about changing careers, or you may be considering going back to school. In this period of reflection and consideration, you have a meaningful opportunity to bring those closest to you into your thought process. This is the time to deeply probe their feelings and concerns about how your life might change and, indirectly, cause theirs to change. It is best to actually make a date for this conversation. It's not a conversation that can just happen and still offer the results you are looking for.

You should schedule a time and meeting place (somewhere special—perhaps in the woods under a big old oak tree) where you are sure there will be no distractions. Give yourselves an uninterrupted two hours. I think you will find, once you start talking, that both of you will have a lot to say and learn.

Before the meeting (or date, since that sounds more intriguing) takes place, both of you should complete the following sentence *in writing:*

I expect the following commitments from my life partner . . .

Some examples of what might be expected are

- ▲ I expect him to spend several hours a day with our children.
- ▲ I expect him to be home on the weekends.
- ▲ I expect him to go with me to see my mother.
- ▲ I expect him to walk the dog.

And in a similar way:

- ▲ I expect her to take off from work if there is a problem at home.
- ▲ I expect her to keep our home clean and presentable at all times.
- ▲ I expect her to be able and ready to travel with me as my business demands.
- ▲ I expect her to be a mother first.

Give yourselves plenty of time. This list should be as thorough as possible. No fair coming back later and saying you forgot something!

Once you feel that your list accurately reflects your expectations of your partner, make a copy of the list and take both copies with you on your date. At the agreed-upon hour and place, you'll need a volunteer to go first. The person going first should give the other a copy of his or her list and take approximately twenty minutes to walk through it, explaining each entry in detail and talking about why each expectation is so important—or why it really isn't, after all. Sometimes we find that we have certain expectations because that's the way it's always been. We've come to count on something because it's familiar and comfortable, but it's not really crucial.

While one person is talking about his or her list, it is important for the receiving partner to just listen. No questions, conversation, or arguments. Just listen. Let your partner tell you, without interruption, what is expected and why. Understanding the reasons why is at least as important as knowing what it is, specifically, that you're expected to do.

Once one of you has finished with his or her list, it's the other's turn. Then, after you have each had an opportunity to explain your lists, but before you start to discuss what you have heard, take a moment to consider which expectations you could give up. If you couldn't have them all, which are the least important to each of you?

Now it's time to talk about what you have shared with each other. How do you feel about what your partner expects of you? Were you surprised at the expectations? Are they what you anticipated? What are the expectations that are in jeopardy of not being met if you go forward and make a change in your life? What other decisions must you make to reconcile what you want to do with the needs of your partner? Will your partner make some adjustments? Each of you should ask these questions of yourself and share your answers with the other.

> *Men of quality are not threatened by women of equality.*
>
> Zandra Maffett Fennell
> Director, Professional Services
> MacNeil Consumer Products

Try to distinguish between those items on the list that will not be affected by any decision you make and those that will be greatly affected. For example, if you start your own business, being able to travel on demand might be tough or impossible. Those are the items you want to zero in on, the seemingly irreconcilable ones. Remember, though, that there are usually more than two alternatives. Give yourselves the time and space to see all the ways there are of reaching a workable solution that both of you can live with.

You can do this exercise with your kids, too. It may be that you don't often ask your children's opinions on serious issues like this. If you do, though, they'll appreciate it and find it easier to give you their active support, even if the change you're considering means they'll have to lower their expectations from you. They'll understand their role in helping you—*all* of you—to be successful. It will allow them to see, in black and white, how much they ask you to do and how much you do already for them. It will allow them to see what you need to ask of them and why. And it will provide you with some real quality time, listening to each other and sharing your feelings.

I have found that if I understand why you are doing something and what it means to you and to me, I am much more likely to be helpful, as opposed to sitting on the sideline and having my imagination run wild. I firmly believe that you need to explain to your kids why this change is so important to you, what you're feeling, and that, no matter what happens, you love them more than anything else. Don't put them in a position where they see you doing all this other stuff, starting a business or whatever, changing their lives, and just assume that through all those changes they will realize that you still love them. It doesn't work that way. Kids need extra assurance.

Ask them the same questions you asked your life partner. What are the most important things to them? What wouldn't they mind giving up? Talk about all of their feelings and about yours. Believe me, they want to know how you feel and why you want to do whatever it is you are considering. They want to know they didn't do anything wrong. Take the time with your kids, one by one, talking and listening and sharing. You won't regret a minute of it.

At the end of each of these conversations, take some time to simply reflect together upon what you've just done and what you've learned from it. If you are like a lot of people, it may be the first time in a long while that you have devoted uninterrupted time to this kind of sharing.

In other words, keep talking. Do it yourself, but don't do it alone.

9

Body of Knowledge: The Physical Lifescape

THE BODY HAS ITS OWN WAY OF KNOWING, A KNOWING THAT HAS LITTLE TO DO WITH LOGIC, AND MUCH TO DO WITH TRUTH, LITTLE TO DO WITH CONTROL, AND MUCH TO DO WITH ACCEPTANCE, LITTLE TO DO WITH DIVISION AND ANALYSIS, AND MUCH TO DO WITH UNION.

—MARILYN SEWELL

WHEN YOU STARTED thinking about running your own business, I'd guess there's a good chance that you didn't give too much thought to your body in relation to your decision. It's an important part of the equation, and not to be taken for granted. Being a business owner makes your physical welfare take on a new importance.

When you work for someone else, you think about your personal health and body differently. Your health insurance is often paid for. There are sick days and you use them, staying home to take care of yourself.

When you're running your own business, sick days often appear to be an impossible luxury, especially if you're running it alone. Even if you have partners or employees, you often have the thought that if you aren't there, then no one's going to "mind the store" the way you would. You frequently cancel doctor appointments so you can make that important presentation or otherwise manage every minute of what could be a critical phase for your business. And every phase seems critical, so you just keep driving yourself.

All of this adds up to a tendency to neglect your health. But, as a business owner, how well you take care of yourself has a direct influence on your success. You have to be able to perform consistently at a high level, so you have to be in shape, physically and mentally. You have to know your body, its needs and capabilities. On the most basic level, all you have is your body, mind, and soul. Taking care of yourself adds to your energy, enthusiasm, and level of alertness, and those are important parts of the success equation.

So it's going to be absolutely essential that you do take good care of yourself. Owning a business has reinforced for me how important it is that I remain physically fit. The business's prospects would change dramatically if I were out of commission for any length of time.

> *Never lose the vision, but remember to pace yourself.*
>
> Renee Steiger, Owner
> Takeout Taxi of South Jersey

Not that I'm indispensable, or that I don't have very competent people working with me. It's just that I am a driving force for our business, so the thought of getting sick or of simply not having enough energy scares me in a way that it never did when I was an employee. The negative impact it would have now is much bigger and more far-reaching.

Of course, being healthy was always important. But whenever there was a conflict between a business meeting and a doctor's appointment, it was always the doctor's appointment that got canceled. Well, no more of that for me . . . or for you!

Whatever your new direction ends up being, you're going to need good health and boundless energy to make a success of it. And there's absolutely no reason for you to put off doing something about it until you've decided what it is you want to do, either. This is the kind of action you can take to begin practicing investing in yourself.

So get out your calendar or appointment book, and let's do something absolutely absurd. Let's not pencil in but schedule with a pen those investments you're going to start making in yourself that relate to your health.

First, I'd like you to actually mark down times to sit down and eat three good meals a day. You know what good meals are. Put them in your calendar: breakfast, lunch, and dinner.

Second, we all need a certain number of hours of sleep to perform well. However many hours you need—and be honest—go on and mark it down. Personally, I need eight hours.

Lastly, you need to do something physical every day. Everyone has a preference. I like to walk or ride my horse. (My doctor contends that the only way that horseback riding is exercise is if I carry the horse; obviously, he's never ridden!) It doesn't matter much what it is, as long as you do it regularly. Right now, schedule at least five hours of some sort of physical exercise into your week. If the president of the United States can find time to jog, you can work some regular exercise into your schedule.

There's still going to be time for your family, your friends, your work, and all the rest, but you must be determined to do *at least* this for yourself, every day. This is the minimum. Practice this discipline for a couple of weeks, and you'll see that it *is* possible to make it part of your life from now on.

If you find that there is no way you can do the things you just marked on your calendar, do not, I repeat, do not, even consider starting a business. I am absolutely serious.

And you must start *now* because you will greatly increase your chances of success if you master this skill before jumping into business ownership, a new job, a new profession, or a new life. It's a prerequisite to success, not an afterthought.

Thinking with Your Body

There are a lot of reasons for taking your physical being into account in making your decision. Some of them have to do with the ways in which your physical being has a direct effect, good or bad, on the way you work and how effective you are in your work. In your journal, write a few paragraphs about yourself in response to the following questions:

Can you work for long hours without interruption, or are you most efficient when you're able to take regular breaks? How frequent and how long do those breaks have to be?

Are you a morning person, or does it take a while for you to get revved up to full speed? Do you even prefer to work at night? What time of day is your thinking most clear?

Are you prone to frequent illness or physical manifestations of tension? How would you describe your energy level? Would you describe yourself as generally active or inactive?

How careful are you with your health? What do you do to preserve it? How many times did you go to a doctor or dentist last year?

It is extremely important that you understand your body and its needs in order to perform at the highest level of which you're capable. Thomas Edison used to take frequent catnaps at his laboratory. He was in touch with his body and knew what he needed in order to optimize his creativity; and look at all that he accomplished. Diana Vreeland would have a shot of Scotch and a peanut butter sandwich for lunch every day. I'm not advocating drinking at lunch, but the point is that she knew what worked for her.

Other considerations have to do with the kind of working conditions you prefer. Numerous studies show that work environments have a significant effect on people's productivity, and that each person reacts a little differently. In your journal, respond to these questions:

Do you like to move around a lot in your work, or do you find that that hurts your concentration? Do you need a big space, or are you more comfortable in a cozy, well-organized office?

Do you need to spend a lot of time outside in order to be content with the shape of your days, or doesn't it matter much to you? Would you like to be working outside at least part of the time?

Do you like a lot of noise and traffic to keep your juices flowing, or do you require quiet? Do you crave contact with other people, or are you perfectly happy to spend your days having them no closer than the other end of a telephone line?

All of these questions have a direct bearing on whether or not a particular business or other sort of activity makes sense for you. All of them are worth giving some thought to. You're trying to fashion an ideal life for yourself, after all, so why not try to ensure that you're going to enjoy it in every respect?

Your Ideal Work Environment

I'd like you to look back at what you've just written, and then describe in your journal your *ideal* work environment. Think about all the factors that will have an impact on your energy level, your productivity, your ability to concentrate, your enjoyment of each day. Imagine your ideal office or other kind of workplace in great detail. *See* yourself working in it and loving it. Where are you?

It's important to be happy in your work space; it can make a huge difference in how productive you are and the way you tackle what needs to get done. If you're having difficulty identifying what your ideal work space would be like, think about the spaces that you have worked in or visited over the years. How were they different from one another? Where were you most comfortable and where did you feel most like yourself?

A woman I met who had bought a business said to me, "I could never work in an environment with fluorescent lighting and no windows." When I was in Corporate America, I just accepted fluorescent lighting without even thinking about it! The point is to *really* think about it. If, after doing so, you can honestly say that your physical surroundings do not affect you, then you have one more point of reference. On the other hand, if you determine that your physical surroundings are important to you, then you can begin to formulate ideas about what you would like to incorporate into your ideal work environment.

Interpreting the Physical Evidence

From another perspective, there are countless stories about men and women who came up with business ideas because of some aspect of their physical being. Susan Powter changed her life by becoming more fit and more self-confident and went on to become one of today's most successful motivational spokespersons. The Mothers Work line of maternity clothes for working mothers was started by a woman who didn't like the merchandise she found on the market. Sheri Poe, a runner, felt the same way about women's running shoes, and founded Ryka, Inc. in order to design and produce a better model. You can find the same kind of stories in the product development departments of many corporations.

I've known such business owners myself. For instance, there was one woman in the process of starting a business with whom I'd talked many times over the telephone before meeting in person. Her business idea involved marketing garments to petite women. Well, when I finally had the occasion to meet her, I saw just how perfect this business was for her, and I understood something about the passion for her new business that I'd heard her express over the phone. She's under five feet tall, and her physical qualities, her personal understanding of the market, were going to give her a competitive advantage in serving that market. She *was* the market!

Let me give you an example of just how powerful our differences can be in creating competitive advantage. Have you ever seen that hair gadget that enables you to make an inverted ponytail? It's called the Topsytail. Do you know what the inventor's competitive advantage is? Dyslexia. She liked the twist in Meg Ryan's hair in the movie

When Harry Met Sally . . . and went home to try and do it herself. She couldn't, at first, but then decided to invent a tool to do it. She realized she needed a way to make a reverse ponytail—a realization she attributes to being used to seeing things in an inverted manner, because she has dyslexia. She's built the Topsytail Company into a $40 million business. That's quite a competitive advantage.

I'm not suggesting that *you* will necessarily get your next business opportunity out of your physical lifescape. I am simply suggesting that you should look at your entire being for answers. Our insights and discoveries come from our own experiences, and we experience much of life from a physical perspective.

What we're going to do now may feel a little bit like going to the doctor's office. You know: The nurse hands you a clipboard with dozens and dozens of questions attached to it, and says, "Could you give us a quick update?"

Some of my questions will require only one-word answers from you while others may require a paragraph. Any one of them might provoke a thought that *could* be the key to your business. They're deliberately somewhat random, because I want to encourage you to free-associate with them. While you're going through them—with your journal in hand—write down everything you are feeling or thinking in response to them, any mental associations they give rise to, any memories or ideas that come to mind.

By the way, you might want to do this exercise with a friend or even with your kids. It can be fun and a good way to laugh, and that's one of the best ways of keeping fit I know of. Looking at the choices we make having to do with our physical selves often tells us about our decision-making in other spheres. Are there any conclusions you can draw about the rest of your life from how you are responding to these questions? As you answer these questions, also write down any problems that you've experienced by virtue of who you are physically: never being able to find the right size, trouble finding a partner for your chosen sport, finding the type of food you enjoy, stuff like that. You may be looking at an incredible opportunity. Just take note of it for now.

1. What is your height?
2. How would you describe your weight to someone else? What does the scale say? How do you reconcile the two?
3. Some people have the physique of a swimmer, some of a gymnast. What is yours like? Define in terms of a sport.
4. What is your favorite food?
5. George Bush hates broccoli. Hillary Clinton hates peas. What do you hate?
6. What do you consider to be your best feature?
7. What physical activity do you enjoy above all others?
8. When was the last time you broke into a sweat? (Excuse me, perspired!) What caused it?
9. If you could pick whether to go to a manicurist, a masseuse, a physical trainer, or a chiropractor, which one would you choose?
10. How would you describe how you look most days?
11. If you are not going to work and you are not going to see anyone, what time do you take a shower and get dressed?
12. Do you wear makeup every day?
13. If I had the opportunity to meet you, what would be the first thing that I would notice about you?
14. Do you consider yourself coordinated?
15. Describe what you will look like when you are seventy years old. Will you be active or taking it easy?
16. On a scale of one to ten, ten being the highest, how important is having an intimate relationship to you?
17. What was your all-time favorite hairstyle?
18. What animal do you look like?
19. Do you have any special physical capabilities that you rely on or use regularly?
20. Do you have any physical capabilities that hold you back?
21. Do you wear glasses or contact lenses?
22. What part of your physical makeup makes you so special?

23. If you could change one thing about yourself, physically speaking, what would it be?
24. Which of the five senses is most important to you? Which one would you give up, if you were forced to?

At this very moment, I want you to hold that thought I know is in your head ("this woman is crazy"), close your journal, and go take a walk. I don't care if it's on a treadmill. I just want you to get up and go walking.

While you are doing this, I want you to think about how walking feels. Does it add to your sense of well-being, or do you feel it's a waste of time? I also want you to think hard about what physical abilities and characteristics you have that make you special, make you unique. Keep walking until you have formulated a new perspective on how your physical sphere might be instrumental in helping you to discover what it is you love to do.

Putting It All Together

Now do some top-of-mind brainstorming around all the aspects of this sphere I've discussed. What actions would you like to take in terms of your physical being, especially your health? Are there any business ideas that come to mind? If you don't end up starting your own business, what do your preferences concerning your work environment indicate that you should do instead?

Here's what some other women have come up with:

> I know that if I don't take care of myself physically, my energy level totally dwindles. I seem to be so sporadic in terms of the way I take care of myself. I'll exercise consistently because I'm getting low on energy, and then I'll drop off because I'm starting to feel better. I'd like to even out my schedule, and eliminate the peaks and valleys.

When I reflect back on the staff job I had several months ago, I didn't realize how drastically the fluorescent lighting and cubicle-style layout affected my moods. Now that I'm out in the field doing sales, I just seem to be in a better mood more often. I really like being out and about, not stuck behind a desk all day.

While I enjoy exercising, I can't always get to the gym on a regular basis. I've let my gym membership run out because I can't justify spending a high monthly fee when sometimes I get there only three or four times a month. I wish I could work out in a gym where you could just pay per visit. I wonder what kind of market there might be for something like that?

Go ahead and see what you come up with. This isn't somewhere we usually look for answers when it comes to making the big decisions in life, but you never know. Some of the answers you're looking for may be right there in you.

10

The Real Bottom Line: The Money Lifescape

MONEY CAN BE TRANSLATED INTO THE BEAUTY OF LIVING, A SUPPORT IN MISFORTUNE, AN EDUCATION, OR FUTURE SECURITY. IT ALSO CAN BE TRANSLATED INTO A SOURCE OF BITTERNESS.

—SYLVIA PORTER

MONEY IS AS much a part of our lives and our ability to live the life we choose as the air we breathe. We cringe when we hear that. It feels like it shouldn't be that way. But it *is* that way, and that's why money is so wrought with emotions. Money is money and a whole lot more.

The ability to earn money means different things to each of us. It can mean that you have accomplished your goals. It may represent having the freedom to rely on yourself. It may stand for a certain status. It may be the thing your self-worth hangs on. It may be the thing that sets you apart from others in your own mind. It can be all this and more because money represents a whole lot more than an exchange medium. It is security, peace of mind, stability. Like it or not, it touches on everything we do in life, everything we want out of life.

Money provides increased ability to choose what we can do with our lives, today and tomorrow. On the other hand, money can buy *us*—we can sell it our health, our time, our relationships—or at least, that's how we sometimes act. Many of us look at money and think "More is better," while others believe that money is the root of all evil. Judgments are continually passed on individuals on the basis of the size of their pocketbooks. We often judge ourselves in the same way.

I have only one point that I want to hammer away at in this chapter, about money and your relationship to it: Know what it is to you. Know how you think and feel about money. Know what it means to you, to your emotions, to your view of yourself. And understand what a change in your current status, whatever that entails, will do to affect your current equilibrium. This is one of those essential first steps that you *must* take. I am convinced that if every person who considered starting a business looked at her relationship to money as one of the first preparatory steps, our overall success rates for business start-ups would increase significantly.

> *To be in business you must generate a profit; otherwise, it's called volunteering.*
>
> Susan W. Antal
> M.S. Antal & Associates

If you have been considering business ownership for a while or are already a business owner, you have probably come across one of the many existing checklists on things to do when starting and growing a business. Among the points to consider, there is invariably some question such as "Can you live without a salary for twelve to eighteen months?" Any business consultant or accountant will encourage you to analyze your savings, your monthly expenses, your expected cash flow, and what and who you have to fall back on should the unexpected arise. These are important preparatory steps for creating and running a successful business and shouldn't be skipped.

The question misses the entire point, however, as to why you should look so closely at your relationship to money, cash flow, expenses, and savings. Remember Donna? Her business was doing great from the start, she had all the cash she needed, but the uncertainty was unbearable to her, and it finally drove her right out of business ownership. Donna's reaction was hardly unique.

I once worked with a woman who'd decided to start a business after she was "reorganized" out of her corporate position of twenty years. She had over *half a million dollars* in savings, and since the business she started didn't require a large cash outlay to get it up and going, that money was basically available to her for living expenses and "fall-back" money. She'd worked hard and been a real saver, so it wasn't luck that got her to where she was.

She'd been in business for almost three months when I visited her one day and noticed a calendar on her desk filled with red hashmarks and circles. I was intrigued. A new system of some kind? Her answer blew me away.

The calendar was her record, on a cumulative basis, of how many days she had worked without earning any money! She updated it religiously every morning. In fact, it was the first thing she did. She was obsessed with it, convinced that she would end up a bag lady if she didn't start earning money . . . soon! This, after only three months! Well, it wasn't too many months later that she threw in the towel.

When you change a person's earnings, you are going to alter her perception of herself and her situation. I think that's true for everyone. We might not like to hear that, might prefer to think it's not true of us, but there's no way around it: There *will* be emotional fallout.

The big question is not whether you *can* live for twelve to eighteen months without a salary: It's how you're going to *feel* about not earning any money over an extended period of time. How are you going to feel about *yourself* and your future, with money going out for day-to-day living expenses and as investments in the business but with nothing coming in for a while?

The ability to deal with such feelings of uncertainty during the first few *years* in the life of a new business is a "must-have" in your survival kit. It may be more important than the actual cash.

Before you spend hours calculating cash flow and monthly expenses, make sure you understand *your relationship to money*. It's a more appropriate investment of your time and one that guarantees a higher payback.

What Is This Thing Called Money?

ONLY IN GROWTH, REFORM, AND CHANGE, PARADOXICALLY ENOUGH, IS TRUE SECURITY TO BE FOUND.

—ANNE MORROW LINDBERGH

I know a doctor whose dad died of a heart attack at a relatively young age: consequently, my friend feels that he, too, will die young. Because of that conviction, he literally spends every dime he earns. He's very successful, makes a ton of money, but he doesn't have any savings to speak of. Emotionally, he just doesn't need it. What he needs is to live every moment as if it were his last. He is locked into the present, and money for him is a means to live every minute of it with gusto.

This man points to a certain event—his father's death—as the reason why he is the way he is. His mother, however, says he was always like that, and I have a hunch she might have the inside scoop on this one. Life is not generally so simple. I believe that we each have a tendency toward a particular type of relationship to money that we are comfortable with; as a rule, we don't change that relationship very easily. Our situation may change, but how we feel about money seems to be relatively fixed.

There are no good types or bad types, either. There is only the need to recognize what money means to you and to use that knowledge to determine the life choices that fit your emotional template.

Exchange Value

Have you ever noticed how little we really talk to each other about money, even though it often seems we're talking about it all the time? Sure, we'll tell trusted friends if we're having money worries. We'll talk about how we need more of it or about how we earn it or plan to earn it. We don't usually go much deeper, though.

It's almost as if there's some sort of taboo concerning money, not unlike the taboos that surrounded the subject of sex for so long. And, even though most of us talk about sex much more openly than anyone did a couple of generations ago, money is still very much off-limits. It's not hard to see why, either, when you consider all those personal and societal meanings that get attached to it: money is perhaps the greatest source of anxiety there is.

I'd like you to try to break through some of the taboos. I'd like you to turn to your mirror circle and your "I believe in you" person to discuss the issues that come up for you as you do the exercises in this chapter. This is very important to your ability to get a true picture of what money has come to mean to you. Here as elsewhere, talking with others can help you to see yourself in new ways. It can show you that you're not alone in the way you feel, and it can suggest attitudes and strategies you might want to adopt as your own.

> *Creating a successful relationship with money is like creating a successful personal relationship. You have to be willing to invest and divest.*
>
> Rosemarie Greco
> President and CEO
> CoreStates Bank

Your discussions can begin on a very basic level. For instance, they can proceed from sharing simple facts. As an example, I've occasionally learned that couples I know don't have joint checking accounts. I find this kind of intriguing, although there's certainly nothing wrong with it. I just wonder what it says about how each person feels about money, and how those feelings interact in the life of the couple. I've had some fascinating, revealing conversations come out of that one fact.

And the point *is* to get beyond the facts, to what goes on with you *emotionally* when it comes to money. If you can do that with your mirror circle and your support person—exactly *because* money is such an intimate subject—you'll be able to free up your private thoughts all the more.

That's why I'm not going to say at any particular point, "Go talk with these people now." I want you, instead, to react to what's happening in the exercises and enrich the experience as much as you can by consulting with others. Especially when you come to points where you feel blocked or feel uncomfortable with what you're learning, ask for help. It's a good rule for this whole process; it's particularly good when you're dealing with a subject that most of us don't like to look into too closely.

Money and Your Feelings

People tell me all the time either that they are going to start a business in order to get rich or that money doesn't really mean much to them, and they're starting their business in order to make a contribution. Neither of those statements says anything about their true relationship to money, though. Each statement focuses on an *outcome;* money's *meaning* for you will affect you long before you get close to any financial outcome you anticipate from your business.

Imagine what it would feel like if your regular paycheck was suddenly gone. Don't worry about whether that's even in the cards; try to forget about the practical considerations, even: just tune in to your feelings. Does the mere thought of it scare you to death, or do you feel that everything would be okay? Are you feeling confident or destroyed inside?

Give it a few minutes. Try to experience, as vividly as you can, being in such a situation. When you've succeeded and stayed there for a while, seeing how it feels, open your journal. Capture the feelings you experienced during your imaging work.

NOW I'D LIKE you to explore what underlies your emotional reactions to that imagined situation: namely, your thoughts and feelings in general about money. Do you think about it every day, hardly ever, or somewhere in between? Are your major concerns with the future or the present? Is what you have never enough, or is there a certain amount above which you no longer worry? How much is enough, and what do you think that says about your feelings concerning money?

Here are some examples of the types of feelings other women have expressed:

> I feel money gives me freedom, although even when I have money, I don't always feel free.
>
> ---
>
> I feel money is always hounding me. I worry about it all the time. I don't know why. I have some, but that doesn't seem to eliminate my worry. It makes me miserable, to be honest.
>
> ---
>
> Money? I never think about it! I think about living life, doing what I want to do. Sometimes I have it and sometimes I don't. I get by. It's just not that important to me. I feel that it is not worth all the aggravation. At least, not for me.
>
> ---
>
> Having money makes me feel better about myself. It's a tangible piece of evidence that everyone can see. It says I am worth something. I can't imagine not having a lot of money.
>
> ---
>
> I feel surprised about how much they are paying me to do this job. I am not sure I am even worth it. I would probably take less.

If some of your feelings seem contradictory, that's okay: they often are. In fact, they usually are. Right now, you just want to try to get all of your feelings recorded. Don't worry too much about whether you can make sense of it all. This is a good exercise in which to just let loose.

AFTER YOU'VE RECORDED these general thoughts about money, explore the specific, private meanings that lie behind these thoughts. What does money represent to you? Freedom, power, status? Is it merely something you have to have in order to get by? Is it even a nuisance? Is it a means to an end or an end in itself, a measure of your self-worth?

Be very honest with yourself. Money is one of those subjects about which we're "supposed" to feel certain things: there are a lot of values tied to it other than its actual exchange value, and most of us have feelings about money we wouldn't necessarily reveal to anyone else. But your purpose here is not to be judgmental; it's to *know yourself.* Write down everything, as long as it's true.

Finally, do you think of yourself as a saver or a spender? That's not as simple a question as it seems. We all have some general notion of ourselves as savers or spenders, depending on our behavior and how we'd like to behave. The point here is to connect the thoughts and feelings—the various meanings you've discovered—to your view of yourself, in a very direct way. Do you see connections? Conflicts? Be very thoughtful, here. Why do you think you are the way you are with money?

I am prodding you here to think deeply about money in a way that we seldom take time to do. Stripping away all consideration of the actual things that money can buy and focusing on your relationship with money, knowing how you feel about money, provides you with invaluable clues as to how you might fare emotionally through the changes you are considering.

From this viewpoint, what we do with money—how we use it, earn it, think about it, protect it, donate it, spend it, invest it and preserve it—*is nothing more than a metaphor for how we feel inside.* Remember, there is no right answer. There is just the way you are.

Your Money Story

Now I want you to take everything you've just learned into account and write a story. I want you to describe your entire life, using money as the central theme. If you had to tell a stranger who you were, without the benefit of any reference points other than that of money, what would you say?

You are probably saying to yourself, "What is she talking about?" Let me try and get you started with some questions. Write down the answers; pretty soon you'll get the hang of it and be able to put it all together into a story, your story, as seen through the eyes of money.

- ▲ Growing up, how did your parents treat money? Who earned it? Who decided how it would be spent? Saved? Invested? Who managed the money in your home?
- ▲ Growing up, did you feel there was a lot of money around, or did it seem like it was hard to come by? Did you feel poor or rich? Or didn't you care?
- ▲ Was money a source of arguments between your parents? Stress? Worry? Or was it a minor part of your family life, as far as you could tell?
- ▲ Did you have to earn money as a kid? Did you get an allowance? What did you have to do for it? How old were you when you first got what you thought of as a real job?
- ▲ What did you do with the money you earned? Did you pay for your education?

Are there any really memorable experiences that you had concerning money while growing up? Those people who grew up during the Depression were affected by it for the rest of their lives. What about you? Maybe your father lost his job? Or you grew up in a single-parent home?

I worked with one woman who grew up without her father. Her mother did everything she could to support the family, but it was tough. This woman recalls vividly how her mother would not allow her to leave the water running while she was brushing her teeth. She and her brothers had to put their toothbrushes under the faucet, get them wet, and turn the water off until they were ready to rinse.

That had an extraordinary impact on her: she knew that she would never allow herself to be put in that kind of position once she was an adult. Today, she is a successful professional who is 100 percent self-supporting. Shortly before she got married, she said to me, "I told my husband, I will never need you. I will always want you, but I will never need you. If you need me to need you, to rely on you financially, you are marrying the wrong girl!"

Now continue into your adult life. If you can take the story from the time you were a kid to where you are right now, that would be great! The more complete you can make it, the better. We are looking to tie facts to the impressions and feelings you just explored.

WHEN YOU'VE FINISHED, I want you to step back and think about what this story says about how you are living your life today and why. There are some incredible learnings in there: let's see if we can find them and codify them.

Read the story you have just written, out loud—it helps you to see the story unfold in your mind. It lets you hear the feeling in your voice. It makes you slow down, think about what you've written, and see *yourself* in the words.

As you read the story, think about the following question: What are the most important things you have come to *believe* over the course of your life about money and your relationship to it? The answer is there, in the story.

After you've finished reading through it, write down your key beliefs. Here are some examples of beliefs that people I've worked with have discovered:

> I associate having money with never having to return to the life I had as a kid. No matter how much I get I will always want more and, you know what, I am unable to part with any of it. I may seem selfish but I am protecting myself. It's just something I have to do.

> I learned a long time ago to put money in the right perspective. My mom and dad did what they loved to do. They weren't what you would call ambitious. At least, not in the sense we

think of it today. But it was worth whatever we missed out on by not having a lot of money. We shared a commitment to living. I would never be doing what I am doing, what I love, if I had been burdened with a need to make a lot of money. I thank my parents every day for that gift.

I have come to believe I am cursed. Everything makes me call into question this fixation, this worrying mentality, I have with money. I have learned I cannot change it. It's a part of me that I have just learned to live with. But I hate it.

I have learned that I just feel better about myself when I have money. When I don't have it, I am really down on myself. I try to avoid that situation at all costs. I used to say that my daily consulting fee was $1200 a day and then quickly add, "But I'll take less!" Now I tell them that I charge a flat $1500 per diem plus expenses. I need to do that for myself. The difference financially isn't that much, but emotionally, it makes all the difference in the world to me and my survival. I am sick and tired of being invisible.

You can tell from these quotes that the output from this exercise can be a real wake-up call. Think hard about your own beliefs, and write them down. Be as insightful and honest as you can be.

Your Most Important Partnership

PEOPLE CHANGE AND FORGET TO TELL EACH OTHER.

—LILLIAN HELLMAN

We need to address the question of what money means in the context of your relationship with your "significant other," if you have one. Your decision is going to affect your net worth; it's also going to affect your relationship, probably in ways that neither of you have anticipated. Any marriage counselor will tell you that money problems are probably the single greatest source of serious, ongoing tension between couples.

To get a really honest dialogue going with your partner about your relationship and your plans for your future together, there's probably no better place to start than on the question of money. So if you have a life partner and you haven't yet discussed, very seriously, very concretely, what your opening a business is going to mean for the two of you—not just financially, but interpersonally, as a consequence of the financial changes that are going to come—then it's time you did.

Considering the subject, this may not be the easiest conversation the two of you have ever had. When life partners are talking about money, it's very easy for them to fall into conflict. In any relationship, there are going to be sources of tension, even resentment, having to do with how money gets earned and spent. It goes with the territory. It's part of sharing one's life.

In this exercise, though, I'd like you to try to put aside any baggage the two of you are carrying from the past. I'd like you to concentrate only on the present and, especially, the future. I'd like you to address each other's concerns, but in as relaxed and loving a way as you possibly can.

In fact, I'll even ask you to hold this conversation outside of the house. There's nothing like money worries to make a couple feel hemmed in, and I don't want you to feel hemmed in. Get some fresh air, take a walk together, find the tree you sat under for that earlier conversation. Make this an open, pleasant, loving discussion.

Here are some questions you might want to ask each other:

> Do you see your current financial situation as enabling or as a barrier to achieving what you want to achieve, personally and professionally, individually and together? What *is* it that you each want to achieve?
>
> You have a life together that's to some extent already set—meaning, you have certain ways of doing things, certain things

that you agree should be part of your life. Making a change, however, may very well involve altering the picture, perhaps radically. What is changeable? Are *both* of you going to be comfortable with changing your lifestyle?

Focus on the specific behavioral changes that would be required. How sure are you that you can live with them? Are you sure you can act out those changes, or do you feel that it is only wishful thinking to imagine that you will be able to make the necessary adjustments? Do your best to bring the discussion down to reality, in financial terms: "This is what it looks like: we need to save this amount of money, which means we might have to give up this and this and this. Can you live with that?"

What are the make-or-break issues? What is untouchable in your current life? What are you not willing to give up as part of the life you envision? How far are you both willing to go, before you won't feel comfortable going any farther? Are you going to need to do some negotiating?

It's not at all uncommon for life partners to have very different feelings about money, and it's best for those differences to be out in the open. How can you help each other to be comfortable with the change you're considering, knowing how each of you feels?

You have to agree, going in, that this is a conversation about the future. Recriminations aren't going to help. If you find yourselves rehashing old arguments, stop yourselves.

On the other hand, don't be surprised if this exercise brings forth some feelings that you weren't aware of. Money is something we don't always talk about openly even with the person who's sharing our life. One of my clients did this exercise with her husband. The next day she called me and said, "This was the first time I really communicated with my husband in almost twenty-five years!"

At a certain point in their discussion, the two of them decided to work up a net worth statement. "First, he didn't see the point," she told me. "*He* knew what we were worth. Then, *I* couldn't believe how much money we didn't have. He was ready to explode because he said he's been telling me for twenty-five years that I was spending all the money! I thought we were going to kill each other . . . but we worked our way through it."

The conversation that ensued made them realize things about their relationship that they'd never known. It went far beyond a discussion of money, too; money was just the impetus for sharing unspoken thoughts on many aspects of their life together. It can be for you, too.

The Bottom Line

Now I want to pull together all the work that we have done in this chapter: your feelings about money, your early learnings about money, and your key beliefs about it. I'd like you to write a short, summary description of your relationship to money.

In putting together your "money type" summary, honesty with yourself is the first requirement. The second requirement is depth in the analysis. Let me give you an example of a "money type" description that has depth, given to me by a woman who was thinking about starting a business:

> When I was growing up my father never had time for me. He was always out earning a living. That was his excuse, anyway. He preached competitiveness to me. Winning was everything. I always wanted to gain his approval, so I did the one thing that I thought would get me that—I went out and earned a lot of money as soon as I graduated from college.
>
> Ever since, money has been my scorecard. I remember my friends saying to me that they thought that I would do anything for money. Anything. That wasn't true and I knew it, but that is how I spent all my time, earning money, so I could see why they thought that.

> Now, after years of earning big-time dollars, I can't seem to put myself in a position where that scorecard isn't my god. I am driven to earn money. I don't need to be so driven anymore—but I guess it's just me. It makes me feel like I am worth something. I know I would be very uncomfortable if I wasn't earning a lot of money. Just the thought of it scares the hell out of me! It's funny, though. The money has nothing to do with my physical needs and everything to do with my emotional survival. Maybe my dad would have been proud.

That is a good, short description of this woman's relationship to money, of what it means to her well-being, and why. It's shorthand for a life that's been shaped in a particular way by this individual's relationship to money.

That's the level of honesty with yourself that we are looking for as you put together a money-type description of who you are.

THE WOMAN WHOSE money-type description I just shared with you did go on to start her own business. She lived without a salary for over a year: an extremely difficult period for her, as you can imagine. Not a day went by when she wasn't fighting herself and worrying about money. She realized from the beginning that she would ultimately do well; however, on most days that didn't keep her from worrying herself sick. She understood, though, what she was *really* worrying about: her scorecard, her father's approval, her own feelings of self-worth. And she did something about it. She went to great lengths during this period to bolster her self-worth in other ways, to compensate for the lack of a visible scorecard.

She has been very successful in managing both her business and her reactions to money. Those first couple of years were quite challenging. Today, it seems to her like they were eons ago.

So you see, your psychological relationship to money will not in and of itself determine whether business ownership is the right choice for you. Money is just one aspect of your life, money considerations just one part of the overall picture when it comes to making your decision. I firmly believe that if the other factors are right, then money problems can and will be overcome by anyone who knows where she wants to go and is passionate about getting there.

11

What You Cannot See: The Beliefs Lifescape

TO LAUGH OFTEN AND MUCH; TO WIN THE RESPECT OF INTELLIGENT PEOPLE AND THE AFFECTION OF CHILDREN; TO EARN THE APPRECIATION OF HONEST CRITICS AND ENDURE THE BETRAYAL OF FALSE FRIENDS; TO APPRECIATE BEAUTY, TO FIND THE BEST IN OTHERS; TO LEAVE THE WORLD A BIT BETTER, WHETHER BY A HEALTHY CHILD, A GARDEN PATCH OR A REDEEMED SOCIAL CONDITION; TO KNOW EVEN ONE LIFE HAS BREATHED EASIER BECAUSE YOU HAVE LIVED. THIS IS TO HAVE SUCCEEDED.

—RALPH WALDO EMERSON

ABOUT TWENTY YEARS AGO, someone sent me those words on a birthday card. I cut the quotation out and put it into a picture frame, and during all the years that followed—as I went from Pennsylvania to New York, to Connecticut, to Illinois, and finally back to Pennsylvania—it went with me.

By now, the picture frame is lined with a permanent film of dust accumulated from offices around the country. That's where it always sat: in my office. I never took it home, because I wanted to have it with me in the place where I *worked*. Emerson was writing about what it means to have a successful *life,* and I wanted to make sure that I never forgot the values he expressed while I was busy building my career.

Today, it sits on my desk at home, displaced from the "workplace" along with me. It's one of the very few reminders of the past that I have allowed into my home.

TIME AFTER TIME, the women business owners I've met over the past several years have told me that it's equally important to them to run their businesses in a way that expresses their values as it is to make a profit. I understand them perfectly because that's exactly how I feel about Capital Rose.

Working for someone else, having to follow their rules, I think too many of us feel far too often that we're supposed to leave our values in the parking lot when we arrive at work. Of course, very few employers would admit that that's what they expect from their employees. But actions speak louder than words, and we've all seen the "it's a jungle out there" mentality at work.

I know the people with that mentality think they're being smart, but I have to say, it's not even what I would call good business practice. It's murder on customer loyalty because sooner or later customers *do* perceive that something is rotten. And it's a continuing source of anger and frustration in the workplace, which is one reason so many of the best and the brightest are striking out on their own. They want to do things *their* way.

Listening to those women business owners talk about the importance of incorporating their own values into their companies, I could see that they'd done some very deep thinking about exactly what it was they wanted from their lives. It's not that they weren't being businesslike in their new ventures. They were putting something extra into the success equation.

They were questioning the old models and constructing new ones that reflected who they were as individuals. Building their businesses around their lives meant that, bottom line, they weren't in it *just* for the money. They were looking to contribute. They were building legacies for their families, their colleagues, their communities. They were seeking the dignity that comes with saying, "This is the way *I* want to do it, and that's how it's going to be done, no matter what."

I've seen this so consistently that I've come to believe women business owners are in the vanguard of a *revolution in values* in terms of the way we do business.

And, despite how difficult the struggle often is, I see countless individuals in the corporate world continually striving to be allowed to express their own values in their work. I've been there, and I know how hard it can be sometimes, but I do think it's achievable and definitely worth it.

> *The true measure of success is not how fast you progress up the corporate ladder or even if you penetrate the proverbial glass ceiling, but rather, the consistent level of integrity you bring to your profession.*
>
> Cynthia A. Conway
>
> Assistant Vice President, Communications Division
>
> Wilmington Trust Company

Whatever your decision turns out to be, I believe it's not only desirable but imperative for you to be able to express your ethical or spiritual values, your beliefs about life, in your work. This is one area where you already know the "answers," deep down. By creating a specific formulation of your values, you can forge a strong connection between those values and your actions in the world more easily. Do that, and you'll achieve the kind of success that's completely fulfilling, no matter where you are.

Finding Your Foundation

> I SOON REALIZED THAT NO JOURNEY CARRIES ONE FAR UNLESS, AS IT EXTENDS INTO THE WORLD AROUND US, IT GOES AN EQUAL DISTANCE INTO THE WORLD WITHIN.
>
> —LILLIAN SMITH

For many people, this is the most difficult part of the lifescape to construct. It's often difficult for us to put our beliefs into words. They're something we just *know*. That's especially true, I think, when it comes to spiritual beliefs. It's in the nature of the spiritual part of our lives that it transcends language.

Personally, I know that I don't know what it really *is*. I don't have a handy, all-encompassing definition. I just know that, for me, it's there. My conscious awareness of the spiritual aspect of life comes and goes, although there are periods when it's a constant. When I feel a need for awareness of it, it can become a big part of my day. When I relegate it to a background position, I'm content to let it stay there. It seems to be there more or less as I need it.

Sometimes I find it hard to deal with my own spirituality. I am not going to attempt to influence yours, nor should I. But I sincerely believe that to the extent it is there for any of us in some fashion, we need to try to understand it in order to allow it to play a greater part in our lives and in the choices we make.

If you adhere to a particular religion, then you probably have a certain way of speaking about this spiritual aspect of your life. That's fine, of course, but that's not necessarily what I'd like you to concentrate on expressing in your beliefs lifescape—or at least not entirely. What I'd like you to try to do here is give voice to what only *you* can give voice to: your own spirit. I'd like you to listen to that voice within yourself.

And if you're an atheist or an agnostic, where others speak of the soul, you might speak of your conscience, your consciousness of yourself, your awareness, your inner being. Whatever you wish to call it, however you conceive it, it's the thing that makes you who you are, a unique individual going through this world in a way that no one else ever did before or ever will again.

NOW I'D LIKE you to get out your journal and take just five minutes to write down your most fundamental personal beliefs about life. Use an egg timer or an alarm clock to time yourself. I really want you to spend no more than five minutes on this.

Your beliefs are like the cells of your body, part of you, always there and functioning. What is it that you believe, no matter where you are or who you are with? What are these constants in your life?

I'll offer a few examples of what some of the women I've worked with have written. A business owner in Pennsylvania wrote:

1. Doing work that improves the world in some way is important to me.
2. Acting in ways that are honest and ethical.
3. Being as fully myself as possible at all times.
4. Not advancing my own career/development at the expense of my family's well-being.

Another woman wrote:

1. We need to be kind to others.
2. I believe that I can do anything I set my mind to.
3. We are responsible for our own happiness.
4. Life should be enjoyed.

As a last example:

1. I believe in God.
2. I am against discrimination of any kind for any reason.
3. I believe that everyone has the opportunity and the chance to matter.
4. I believe each day is a blessing.
5. I believe in myself.

This is one point in the process where I hesitated to give any examples because I truly want you to blaze your own path here. But I decided that these might be useful to you as thought-starters. Now, please take those five minutes and write your own list.

You may want to discuss your beliefs with your "I believe in you" person or with your mirror circle. You may simply want to meditate awhile on them. You might want to do a little more writing. In any case, take some time to consider them from different angles. Ask yourself: What will these beliefs mean in your new life?

How Do You Show What Cannot Be Seen?

Now, using your personal beliefs as guideposts, and using your journal, I want you to explore the reasons why you've settled on these beliefs and not others, the ways in which they influence your day-to-day life, and your hopes for expressing them in the future.

I'd suggest that the best way for you to start would be to go back to your beginnings. What were your early learnings and experiences concerning your spiritual and ethical beliefs? Who influenced you? Who were your role models? Were you raised in a particular spiritual tradition, or was your household not a particularly religious one? Was your spiritual and ethical nature something you thought about early on in life or only later—or even never at all? Why?

As you grew older, were there any turning points in your attitudes about this aspect of your life? Did they come in the form of momentous events or as the result of a gradual evolution? Or has there been little change in them at all?

There's a story here, of course, but as you write about what's happened in your life, I want you to focus primarily on your *inner* experience, not the events themselves. Try to give expression to what's gone on in the inmost part of yourself, as difficult as that may be.

Now, think—and write in your journal—about the place your beliefs hold in your life today. In what ways are they a product of your past? How do they affect your day-to-day life, and how are they affected by it? Are you content with your ability to act according to your beliefs, or are they frustrated in some way by outside influences? Are there changes that you wish you could make in this respect? What kind? What is your vision of the role that your beliefs would play in your ideal future?

These are very deep waters. The questions I've just asked are only starting points; I leave it to you to discover the deeper questions for yourself.

I'M ALSO GOING to leave it to you to design one last part of your beliefs lifescape: some sort of symbolic expression of your most fundamental values. Only you can determine the best way of doing this, and it can take any form you choose. It could be a piece of creative writing: a play, a song, a poem, a letter. It could be a piece of music, a picture, a sculpture, a dance. It could even be an action in relation to another person. The only requirement is that it take a form that is meaningful for you, a form that expresses what's already there, inside.

> *You must create the space in your life to enable your inner guide to share her wisdom, her creativity, her vision, her courage. Unleashed, she is the single most potent resource you have.*
>
> Marilyn O. Sifford
> Organizational Change Consultant

You may wonder, what's the point of this? Why draw a picture or write a poem about something that's so immaterial, so deeply interior? Is this supposed to help me with my decision?

Well, yes, it is. I think this symbolic expression of your values, one that you decide upon and create entirely on your own, can and should play a very important part in helping you to arrive at your decision.

When it comes to this aspect of existence, we're going a little bit beyond our ability to express ourselves logically. At that point where we connect with our values, there's something extra going on, something that can only be shown indirectly—something that has very much to do with the act of creation.

That's why I want you to choose the form of expression. The particular form doesn't matter: what really matters is the act of creation itself. If you really invest your creation with all of your *feelings* about your beliefs, then it will become a living symbol of them. That way, when the time comes for you to make your decision, weighing all the factors at work in all of the six spheres, I'd like you to be able simply to contemplate your creation and see in it those feelings, those ideas, those values that you put into it.

I love this part of lifescaping because it forces me to take time out and work on a part of me that, most days, I tend to take for granted as simply being there. We all have the same excuse: We're all too busy.

But this is a gift to yourself. Take the time to think about your beliefs, to write about them, and to express them to yourself in some tangible way. It's a terrific way to revitalize yourself, to fill yourself with a sense of purpose and meaning, a reservoir of determination, that you are going to carry with you long after you've finished this process.

12

The Past Is Your Springboard

YOU NEED TO CLAIM THE EVENTS OF YOUR LIFE TO MAKE YOURSELF YOURS. WHEN YOU TRULY POSSESS ALL YOU HAVE BEEN AND DONE, WHICH MAY TAKE SOME TIME, YOU ARE FIERCE WITH REALITY.

—FLONDA SCOTT MAXWELL

WE'VE GONE FULL CIRCLE, through the six spheres of your lifescape. Look in your notebook: you have charts, pictures, lists, questions and answers, letters, essays, maybe even some clippings and doodlings. We're going to draw together all the thoughts and feelings they represent, by looking at your past. How does it all come together?

Most of us will never write an autobiography, but we have all made incredible journeys. Some have been made with great fanfare, others not, but I have never met a person whose past was not interesting and full of learnings and insights.

Yet I have never been one for focusing too much on the past. What's done is done, right? It's not affecting me anymore. You can't change it, so why bother? What good does it do to rehash all those memories anyway? Let's go forward!

I asked a friend recently about her past. I asked her because I knew there had been much sadness in her life. That's not what she talked about, however, or wanted to remember. Instead, she talked about the things she'd learned, people she'd loved, beautiful memories she had.

Not too long ago, I saw an interview with Elie Wiesel, the Holocaust survivor, author, and human rights advocate, on one of the daily talk shows. He was discussing his book *Night*, based on his memories of the time he spent in a Nazi concentration camp.

Wiesel lost his entire family in the concentration camps. He witnessed death and atrocities the likes of which I find it difficult to comprehend. I was deeply moved as he talked about a past so painful that there were parts of it he could not discuss, even after all these years.

The interviewer asked Wiesel how he was ever able to laugh again, to go on with his life, after seeing what he saw. She thought it was a miracle, not that Wiesel had survived, but that he hadn't lost his sanity! When asked how he'd been able to continue on after such tragedy to live a full and productive life, Wiesel said, "Let me turn it around. After seeing what I saw and living in the shadow of death each day, I have six million reasons to laugh, and be happy and go forward."

The miracle in Wiesel's life has been this ability to go on, to continue to believe in himself, in others, in life, and in God. Listening to him talk, you can hear his past speaking in each eloquent word; you can hear, too, the strength and the love of humanity with which he has risen above and beyond that past. He has taken this terrible experience and created with it a life that is admirable, to say the very least. He is a living example of hope for every human being.

If a past such as Elie Wiesel's can lead him to embrace the future, to create a productive and happy life, I believe it is possible for all of us. The future is open; it allows us to use the past in any way we choose. We cannot change our past, we may not have chosen its course, but it is ours, as surely as any material possession we own. The ultimate decision each one of us must make is this: How will we see the past, and what will it be for us—a chain or a springboard?

Yes, there are things in the past that each of us, if given the option, would have avoided, would never have chosen. There are things that were done to us that we still are trying to forget. But in the *totality* of our memories we can find our values, our reason for being, who we are.

We must accept that the bad stuff shaped us as much as the good stuff. While it can be painful, it can also be liberating to put yourself in a position to choose from *all* of it. I believe that those individuals who can see and feel it all are better equipped to live a future that they want.

Life should always involve discovery. What your past tells you about who you are right now is one of the greatest discoveries you can make. The past can be one of your chief assets. It can help you to know what you want, what you don't want, what you like, what you hate. Through the window of the past you can see what has made you happy, what has made you sad. You can discover why you believe what you believe, how you came about your values.

We're now going to use a technique of mapping your past in terms of the six spheres we've just finished exploring. It's a fairly simple technique, so you can either approach it very simply, as a kind of summary of what's gone before, or use it as a means of looking at those spheres, at the entirety of your experience, in a very deep way before you move on to make your decision. The choice is up to you.

I cannot begin to know what opening this door on the past will mean to you. I have opened my own door and worked with other women doing the same. For me, it was an incredibly rich experience, as it was for many of those women. But your needs and desires, just like your thoughts and feelings, are unique.

Trying to get a handle on your past may be an easy thing for you to do, or the very thought of it may be cause for fear. But we are all perfectly imperfect human beings. I encourage you to get everything you possibly can out of this summing-up, however. It's going to show you the way to your new life.

Locating the Reference Points

The process you are going to use to map out your past is one I call "beaconing." I don't think this is a real word, but it's a perfect description for our work. Beaconing involves looking at your life in chronological order, mapping the highs and the lows. Our purpose in doing this is to look for guidance, for signals, for sources of inspiration. We are looking at old information and experiences in order to stake out a new direction; thus, the notion of "beaconing."

One of the most important benefits of plotting out your life in detail is that it gives you the ability to see how good is often created from bad experiences. As you lay out the map of your life, you may note what might be called a springboard effect: often, our greatest learnings, opportunities, life-changing events, follow our lowest points. That's why we want to pay particular attention to the major swings, the peaks and valleys.

There are three parts to this exercise:

1. First, you're going to list the crucial points in your life: turning points, highs and lows, moments or periods of great achievement and joy, and also of despair. While you're making your list, you're going to take note (in as much detail as you can) of how you felt at the time about what was happening to you and how you came to feel about it as time went on.

2. The next step is to choose the fifteen most significant events from your list and "connect the dots" to bring the details together into a chart that shows the peaks and valleys you've crossed. We will discuss how to set up this chart later in the chapter.

3. Finally, you'll look for the *beacons,* the signals that will help light the way to a new direction for you.

First, I'd like you to spend a good amount of time making your list. We're going to end up using fifteen of these, so you can imagine that I'd like you to come up with many more, if possible. This will undoubtedly take you more than one sitting. Your list should include not only things that everyone would agree were important—a death in the family, an honor won, a major career change—but also things whose true significance perhaps only you can appreciate. I included things like the moment I decided, as a girl, that I wanted to become a nun, and the day years later, as an adult, when I bought the horse I had wanted for so many years. You might include things like

- ▲ Major events in your childhood
- ▲ Your first or last day of high school
- ▲ Your first or last day of college
- ▲ Your first job or some other significant job you've held
- ▲ Your biggest achievements: awards you have won, challenges you have met
- ▲ Your greatest failures
- ▲ Relationships: long-term, short-term, happy ones, not-so-happy ones
- ▲ Your engagement, marriage, or divorce
- ▲ The birth of a child
- ▲ Changes in the lives of your children that have affected you: leaving home, getting married, etc.
- ▲ The day you purchased your first home
- ▲ Deaths of those close to you
- ▲ Places you have traveled
- ▲ Times when you were able to buy something you'd always wanted
- ▲ Times you became interested in a particular hobby
- ▲ Major moves: actual relocations; changes in relationships, jobs, career
- ▲ Major accidents or illnesses; hospitalizations

- ▲ Times of great tragedy or joy
- ▲ Periods of deep depression or sky-high hopes
- ▲ Periods of transition
- ▲ Times you will never forget
- ▲ Things that changed your life forever

This list will get you started. Again, I have found that it is impossible to remember everything that should go on this preliminary list in the first sitting. Record what comes to you now, then leave it alone for a while. Go back through your scrapbooks or any diaries you may have kept. Keep working on pulling this list together until you feel as though you could write your autobiography from it.

> *For a long time, the image of what I wanted to accomplish, what I ached to become, intimidated and stifled me—until I learned somehow (and even now have to keep reminding myself) to accept the wonderful unpredictability of achievement and focus on what really matters, what really satisfies: the act itself.*
>
> Ann de Forest, Associate
> Steege/Thomson Communications

As you compose your list, don't just note the events. Concentrate on how you *felt* at the time, in each case. That's what really counts: not the events themselves but your reaction to them. Jot down a few words or phrases that express what it was really like, subjectively speaking. Later on, these subjective reactions are going to be the keys to interpreting this part of your lifescape.

Remember that we too often sum up our past in a few words that don't truly do it justice. Your past wasn't one-dimensional. It can't be summed up in a few words. That's why you need to look at all these separate moments and not just broadly characterize your past experiences.

What memories are flooding through you as you see your life here before you? When was the last time you saw the whole you? Before we move on to the next step, take some time, too, to record in your journal what it's been like to look back over your life in this way.

NOW, BY A PROCESS of elimination, I want you to choose the fifteen items from your list that you feel are going to tell you the most about your past, individually and in combination. I would suggest that this means choosing the fifteen events that involved the strongest emotional reactions, good and bad. The choice is up to you, though.

Really take some time with this. The only way you're going to find the "right" fifteen items is by being deeply introspective. Work your choices out in your journal if you like.

If some of those fifteen items are events with only a very private meaning, the sort of thing that other people might scratch their heads over, wondering why you think they're such a big deal . . . that's fantastic. Chances are, those are the items that are going to provide you with some of your most important beacons.

Now take a long sheet of paper or tape a number of regular sheets together to make your chart. While you're at it, go get your colored markers.

You're going to place these fifteen most significant events along a time line. First, running along the top of the sheet, leaving plenty of room between each entry, copy out the fifteen events in chronological order:

Date:	9-3-52	8-7-56	10-13-57	etc.
Event:	Married	Big Promotion	Grandma died	etc.

Now take a black marker and divide the paper along its entire length, halfway between the top and bottom. Set up a positive/negative scale along the time line, like this:

Date:	9-3-52	8-7-56	10-13-57	etc.
Event:	Married	Big Promotion	Grandma died	etc.
+10 -				
-				
-				
-				
-				
+5 -				
-				
-				
-				
+1 -				
-1 -				
-				
-				
-				
-5 -				
-				
-				
-				
-				
-10 -				

Now make sure you have six different colored markers. Make a little key in the corner of the time line, assigning one color to each of the six spheres:

Resources
Activities
Relationships
Physical Being
Money
Beliefs

For each of the fifteen events you've recorded, I now want you to come up with six ratings, corresponding to the six spheres, from minus ten to plus ten. Under each event, place six different-colored dots: Each dot will indicate the degree to which your feelings at the time, regarding one of those spheres, were negative or positive. If a particular event was neither positive nor negative in terms of a certain sphere, if it had no impact on you, put the corresponding dot on the dividing line.

As always, you should concentrate on *how you felt.* For instance, just because you had a lot of money at some particular point doesn't necessarily mean that you were content in the money sphere of your life. You might want to put the money dot in the negative range, no matter how well you were doing from someone else's point of view. Think hard, remember what it was like. Get past the event itself, and get back in touch with your actual feelings at the time.

This is very hard work, so take your time with it. If you need to take a break and do it over the course of a few sessions, that's fine.

Look at each of the fifteen events on its own. This time line is the distillation of each of the six parts of your lifescape into one graphic representation, so recall all the thoughts and feelings that arose in you as we went through the six spheres in the previous chapters and use the insights you've gained as you determine what ratings to assign to each event on the time line. And place your marks only when you're *very sure* what six ratings you should assign in reference to each event.

Peaks and Valleys

A WOMAN'S LIFE CAN REALLY BE A SUCCESSION OF LIVES, EACH REVOLVING AROUND SOME EMOTIONALLY COMPELLING SITUATION OR CHALLENGE, AND EACH MARKED OFF BY SOME INTENSE EXPERIENCE.

—WALLIS, DUCHESS OF WINDSOR

Once you have all the events rated in regard to each of the six spheres, connect all the dots of the same color, until you have six wavy lines of different colors running the entire length of the timeline. It might look like Figure A.

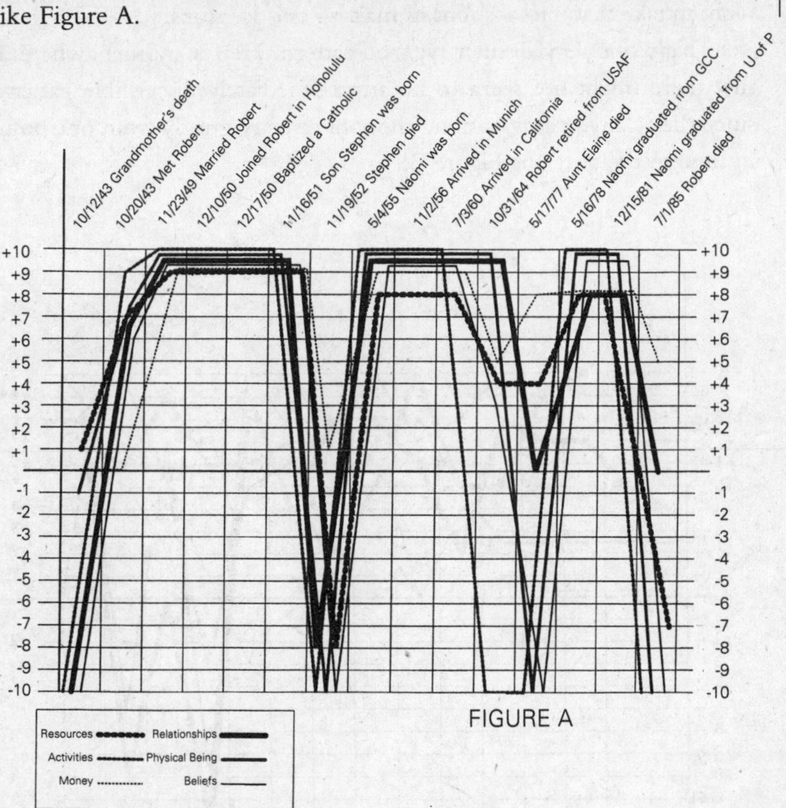

FIGURE A

See how all six lines move, generally, in the same direction at the same time? In a certain sense, a person with this sort of configurations on her time line has six spheres that are highly integrated with one another. We can almost assume that, whenever a couple of spheres of her life improve, the others would be sure to follow. On the other hand, whenever things start to go *bad* in a couple of spheres, it seems that *everything* in this person's life might start going wrong.

This would have certain implications for the person's life. The implications aren't necessarily bad, but this time line does raise questions, for instance, concerning the degree of resilience that this person is able to muster in the face of negative events in her life. She would probably want to take that into account in making her decisions.

That's one very distinct type of pattern. Here's another, where at first there might not seem to be any immediately discernible pattern, since the relative ratings among the spheres vary greatly from one point in time to the next; see Figure B.

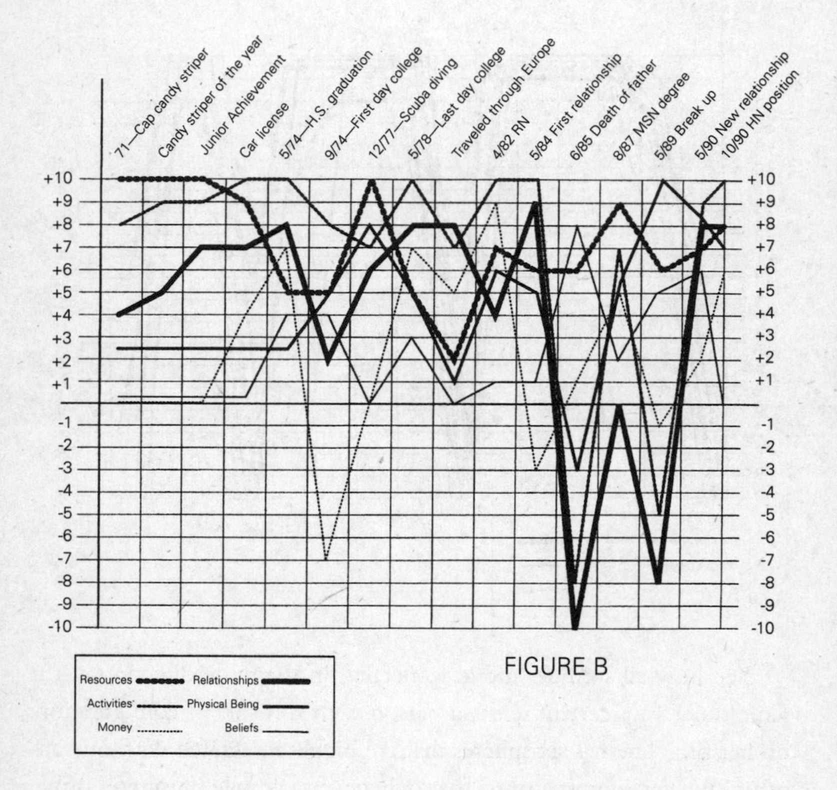

FIGURE B

This is the way most of our lives run. At any time of transition, some things are going well and some aren't, and part of the challenge of dealing with transition lies in the need to deal with that fact.

The key to interpreting this sort of time line is still to look for patterns, though—the only difference being that they're going to take a little more thought to discover. It's not easy. It requires a great deal of thought and self-awareness. But that's how you find the beacons in your time line. That's how you learn things from the past that will prepare you for dealing with transitions in the future. And that's our next step: finding the beacons.

The time line, in itself, doesn't provide answers. Nor does it represent some kind of fated personal response to the events of life; you're not necessarily going to react in the future the way you did in the past. It's a tool for interpreting past events and, most importantly, to the extent that it allows you to reach a greater understanding of your responses to those events, it's a tool for preparing for future action.

Finding the Beacons

I'm about to ask you to do some interpreting and writing concerning the time line you just drew up. First, though, I thought you might be interested to know something about the people whose time lines you just looked at: they belong, in fact, to a mother and daughter who did the exercise together. Here's an excerpt from what Naomi, the daughter, wrote after comparing her mother's time line (Figure A) to her own:

> It was harder than I thought to remember the key events of my life. I was glad that my mom and I decided to do ours together. She tends to remember the order of life whereas I do not.
>
> My life is so different than my mom's. Hers has been so linear. My life has more contrasts than hers. I get back on my feet a lot more quickly than she does. I am grateful that I don't hold on to pain as long as she does.
>
> Now that I'm about to make a major decision in my life, I am reminded by looking at this graph how long it has always taken me to make significant life decisions. Should I return to school to get my doctorate at the age of forty-two? Can I give it my all?
>
> Yes—I always have, towards things and relationships that re-

ally matter. If my past is any indication of my future, I will make a decision when I am ready.

I was surprised to see how everything in one's life doesn't have to be operating at peak levels to accomplish something great. Hey, you know what? I've never had a lot of money during periods of real accomplishment, so maybe I shouldn't worry about having less of it while I'm in school.

As I said, this is just an excerpt. In fact, Naomi went on to write several more pages over the course of many weeks, as she continued to explore what her time line revealed about her. I heartily recommend that you do the same: get yourself started on the search for your beacons, perhaps just by free-associating a little, then keep coming back to your time line to see if any new perspectives emerge on what you see there.

Your thoughts and feelings in response to the time line *are* your beacons: they reveal what sort of things you want to incorporate into your future life and what you want to avoid. Some people are content to express their beacons in the form of paragraphs, as Naomi did, because it allows them to consider many aspects of the data they find all at once. Others like to look for general principles that they can extract and put into a list for easy reference. We all think and learn and use our knowledge in different ways; once again, you should do whatever works for you.

NOW, WHAT DO you see in your own time line? What shape has your life taken?

Are there events where most or all of the six points are above the dividing line? Or below? What about times when it's about half-and-half? How have satisfactions and disappointments in each of the spheres related to each other?

Look at the high points you've marked and think about the similarities and differences between them. Do the same for the low points. What was going on in your life? What was going on in you? What were your feelings? What were your expectations? Were they realized? Is there a common thread as to what gets you to the highs or what causes the lows? Can you explain what happened in between events, right before any of the lines changed directions? Were there things that harbingered the changes?

Look for patterns. They hold the clues to your beacons. Is there anything that jumps out at you, maybe something that you had long ago forgotten? What do these patterns make you think? How do they make you feel?

As you look at this record of your life, you are looking at your invisible assets. Only you can make them visible. Only you can give them prominence in your life.

> *Don't live your life based on what other people might think. You'll never make them or yourself happy.*
>
> Jean Brooks, Director of Advocacy
> Capital Rose, Inc.

You can use the past as your springboard. You can use the learnings and understandings to mold your future in a way that changes the shape of your life. Take some time—a great deal of time, as much as you need—to study your time line. Looking at those highs and lows, remembering what motivated you, what helped you, what strengthened you, what delighted you, you will begin to see the beacons. See your past honestly, and the future you want will begin to come into sight.

PART III

The Road Ahead

13

The Dream Ride: A Path to Yourself

DREAMS ARE . . . ILLUSTRATIONS FROM THE BOOK YOUR SOUL IS WRITING ABOUT YOU.

—MARSHA NORMAN

I LIVE ON A FARM. One of the unexpected pleasures of living there is that, for most of the year, I can count on two or three hot-air balloons appearing above in the early evenings, from I know not where. I love their colors and the faraway feeling they give me. To me they are a symbol of freedom, of a place with no boundaries: they come down to earth to pick you up, and then off you go . . . somewhere . . . soaring, never really knowing where you will end up.

Seeing a balloon on the ground you would never guess how magical it becomes in the air. On the ground, it's not very inspiring. It just lies in a rumpled mess or bobs clumsily, pulling at its tethers. In the air, though, it's where it belongs, right up there with a rainbow, or cumulus clouds, or a pair of turkey vultures coasting on the evening's breezes. It's hard for me to imagine a prettier, more inspiring sight than one of these multicolored balloons gently rising above the treetops at sunset.

So when I asked one of my dearest friends, Marilyn Sifford, who is a highly creative and seasoned organizational change consultant, to write a guided imagery for this book, I was delighted to find that part of the journey takes place in a hot-air balloon. I think that if you've ever taken a balloon ride—or imagined what it must be like to ride in one—you will find this exercise a real treat for your mind and your spirit.

Throughout most of the exercises you've done, we've kept your feet firmly planted on the ground. You've explored many aspects of your life, working to see clearly what *is*. You've also done some imaging work, envisioning what *can be*.

Some people have trouble with imaging exercises. They have a hard time visualizing or think it is frivolous. If you think that way, I understand: there was a time when I probably would have agreed with you. But I'm obviously a convert, and I really urge you to try this one, because it's crucial at this point in the process that you find a way to let go of everyday life and *live in your imagination*.

> *A tree reaches below the surface to gather strength for stargazing.*
>
> Angie Hurlbut
>
> AH Design

If you read through the Dream Ride exercise and just can't bring yourself to do it, then please don't just go on to the next chapter. Find some other way of energizing yourself for what's to come by stimulating your imagination. You might try a modified "Seton Watch" (described in chapter 2), where you just sit still for a while and wait for personal images that accomplish the same things for you that the images in Marilyn's Dream Ride are designed to accomplish: the liberation of your creative energies.

Whatever works for you, do it. Let your imagination soar. Don't worry, we'll get back to earth soon enough. But, first, in order to boost your energy and determination, to allow you to reach within yourself and access all of your resources, I'd like you to dream.

Preflight

There are many ways to reach the resources you hold inside. Different ways work better for different people. The experience in this chapter can be very powerful in tapping into parts of your consciousness of which you are not fully aware.

This experience is entirely unique to the individual. No two even come close to being the same, even though the words of the exercise are the same for everybody. Why? Because each of our imaginations, like our fingerprints, is unlike that of anyone else.

To get the most out of this exercise, you need the following:

- ▲ A quiet place where you will be undisturbed for approximately one hour.
- ▲ Background music to play while you are listening to the guided imagery. New Age instrumental music works best for most people. I especially like the album *Pianissimo* by Suzanne Ciani. However, any smooth, melodic music that isn't distracting can work.
- ▲ A person to read the guided imagery. It will help for the reader to rehearse at least a couple of times, to get a feel for where and how long to pause effectively in order to enable you to get the most out of it.

You cannot do a guided-imagery exercise while reading the script. You can be the reader or a participant, but you can't be both at the same time. If you want to do the exercise alone, which is not unusual, here are several suggestions on how to do that:

- ▲ Practice reading the guided imagery as suggested above, to get the pacing and voice, and make a tape of it. You can then play the tape anytime you want to do the exercise.

- If you think that hearing your own voice may be distracting, enlist a friend to practice and make a tape recording for you. Make sure you pick someone whose voice you are attracted to and find calming.

If you are doing the exercise in a group, select one person as the reader and allow everyone else to participate. If you want to do the exercise more than once and trade off the reader role, that's fine; in fact, it's a great idea. Just make sure that the reader has a chance to practice before you begin the exercise. Stumbling over the words during the reading will break everyone's concentration.

Once you have your cassette tape or your reader and you are ready to go into your own space, dim the lights. Keep your journal close by. You are going to record the discoveries you make. Now, let's begin with a relaxation exercise . . .

Find a comfortable position, either sitting straight with your back well supported, feet flat on the floor and hands in a relaxed position, or, if the setting permits, lying flat on your back. When you are comfortable, close your eyes. Take a few deep breaths and, as you exhale, feel your body begin to relax.

Imagine, floating above you, a beautiful stream of light. This light is a color that is very pleasing to you, and when you are deeply relaxed, the energy of the light flows easily throughout your entire body.

Now breathe the light into your body, and let it flow into every limb and every organ of your body from the top of your head to the tips of your toes. As the light moves through you, feel your entire body becoming deeply relaxed—your feet, the calves of your legs, your thighs, your entire lower body. Continue to breathe deeply and feel the warmth of the light as it flows through your chest, your lungs, and your abdomen. Notice how soothing it feels as it travels through your shoulders, your arms, your hands, your fingers. The light, dissolving tension wherever it goes, is now flowing into your neck, your head, your face, your jaw, until they are all completely and totally relaxed.

The Path to Yourself: A Guided Imagery

Now imagine you are walking down a beautiful, magical path. It's an ideal day to be here. Brilliant sunbeams are streaming through the trees, a gentle breeze caresses your face, bringing with it the earthy and sweet fragrance of the vibrant flowers and lush foliage of every description.

You are keenly aware of being surrounded by nature's gifts: the sights and sounds and sensations of life itself. The beauty and serenity of this setting are uplifting and inspiring and you know that this path will lead you to a very special place.

As you round a curve in the path, you notice a small plaque with these words on it: WELCOME TO THE MAGICAL PATH TO YOUR SELF. This *is* a magical path. Here you can go and see and do whatever you choose. There are no boundaries, no limits, no shoulds, on this magical path. There is only you, with your talents, your wisdom, your experience, your commitment, your imagination—everything you need for this journey. On this path you will be able to create whatever it is you want or need, to have a pleasant and rewarding experience. You may do this by visualizing; or through hearing sounds; you may otherwise sense or feel your surroundings; or you may think about the experiences I suggest. Let yourself experience what comes naturally, and know that however you experience it is right for you.

If I say or suggest anything that produces images that are unpleasant or uncomfortable for you, alter the suggestion to meet your needs; this is *your* magical path.

You have come here to be alone with yourself—to be in touch with the central core of your being—the core that embodies the essence of your true self. This central core is the source of your most powerful energy—your life force. It is unique—one of a kind because you are one of a kind.

When you are in tune and aligned with this central core, the power of your being emerges almost without effort. You are led by your wisdom—by your own way of knowing—from a place deep within you. You are not easily buffeted about by the many competing forces in your world, forces that would have you abandon your own core and thus misuse or give away your power.

As you continue walking down the magical path, you notice a small sign that reads PRIVATE ENTRANCE. You know intuitively that this is the entrance to your secret garden—a peaceful place of your design where you can hear your inner guide and let your own voice emerge. This garden is your private space, and no one enters this space unless they are invited by you.

As you descend the steps leading to your special garden, feel any concerns or distractions melt away, and focus on the question that is central to your life at this point.

(PAUSE)

In the garden you see a small, open book with blank pages. Take a moment to write down your question.

(PAUSE)

Now be still and wait for your inner guide to respond to your question.

(PAUSE)

It is now time to leave your special garden. As you reach the steps, out of nowhere a wise and benevolent old sage appears. The sage smiles warmly, hands you a beautiful box, and then vanishes.

Open the box and take a moment to savor this gift and to understand its significance to your journey.

(PAUSE)

As you continue down your path, you realize that you have rarely been in a place so inspiring and so completely attuned to your needs.

Pause for a moment and look around, notice how you are feeling, the energy within you and around you. As you scan the surroundings, you see something to which you feel particularly drawn. It may be a tree, an animal, a flower, or something else, but there is something about it that feels very powerful to you. Whatever it is, in this magical place, imagine yourself becoming that something. Let yourself be filled with its life force. And for a moment, in this world with no boundaries, let yourself fully experience the innate power of being this new life form.

(PAUSE)

Notice how it feels to move in a different way. Feel the energy of this life form in your body—your senses—your voice—your view and perspective of the world.

Experience the visceral energy as you soar high above the ground, or gallop, or perch, or climb, or plant yourself firmly in the ground, whatever it is that you choose to experience.

(PAUSE TWENTY TO THIRTY SECONDS)

Now, think of a word that describes the essence of this experience to you.

(PAUSE)

As you approach a clearing, let yourself return to your own body. Bring with you the new energy you have discovered in another life form, for it is part of you and you can call on it whenever you choose.

In the clearing, there is a small and beautiful pond. Go over to the pond and look at your reflection. What do you notice about how you look? Can you see this new energy in your reflection?

(PAUSE)

As you prepare to continue your journey, you notice near the pond a giant hot-air balloon. It has come to take you on a very important trip. As with everything in this magical world, you are completely safe with your balloon. It will be guided by your will and automatically go where you, by your thoughts, direct it to go. Now climb into the basket and slowly let it begin to rise.

(PAUSE)

As it rises, you notice there are two packages in the basket with you. One is labeled YOUR SPECIAL GIFTS: FUEL FOR THE JOURNEY. The other package is unlabeled, but you notice it is heavy and burdensome—making it difficult for the balloon to rise, causing you to work much harder at steering its movement—and you wonder why you brought it on this trip.

You'll come back to this one a little later. For now, focus your attention on the package that says GIFTS: FUEL FOR THE JOURNEY.

This package represents *your* special gifts, the parts of you that are alive and well when you experience your most powerful self—at work, at home, with your family and friends, in the community and the world. And there is a gift in this box that represents something that is uniquely you. You will find it in a special velvet pouch.

When you are ready, open the box. Take a moment to savor your gifts.

(PAUSE)

What are the special gifts? And how does it feel to discover these parts of yourself? What is the gift in your velvet pouch and what meaning does it have for you? Own these gifts, know they are a valuable treasure to be honored and nurtured.

(PAUSE)

Now imagine these treasures becoming the energy for your balloon; the supply is plentiful because it comes from your central core, your life force, and it renews itself. It is the source of your power. Feel this energy take over and cause your balloon to rise and move forward more easily.

Yet notice that something is still holding you back. You sense it is the contents of the unlabeled package. This package contains all the things that are keeping you from being your best and most powerful self in the various arenas of your life, things that keep you from creating the life you want and need for your own well-being.

It may include outdated habits, negative attitudes, old hurts or resentments, outdated relationships, self-doubts, or fears—fear of failure, fear of success and what it could mean, fear of the unknown, fear of disapproval, or other fears.

One by one, take those things you wish to leave behind and throw them over the side of the basket, watching each one as it falls from view.

(PAUSE)

What you leave behind can be just as important as what you bring with you, for it is necessary to let go of old patterns that made sense at one time but that no longer work for you, to make way for new ways that make more sense for where you are now and where you are going. Now, as you leave behind this excess baggage and take with you a new appreciation of your special gifts, notice how you are feeling—how easily the balloon glides, responding to your thoughts and steadily moving toward your destination.

You are now ready to journey forward into your future, where you will create an ideal vision of your best self in three arenas of your life: your personal life, your work life, and your life in your community.

As your balloon flies on this beautiful day, the blue sky suddenly becomes a giant screen. Projected onto this screen, bigger than life, are images of you living in the future in these different arenas.

Looking straight ahead, you first see the future of your personal life and relationships. Take a moment to observe what you have created. Notice where you are living—your lifestyle, the people you have chosen to bring with you, the people who are absent, how you are spending your time. Notice how it feels to be living your life in a way that is truly aligned with who you are.

(PAUSE)

On the corner of the screen there is a small and beautiful one-room house. The house was put here to provide a special place for you to have a conversation that you need to have with one of the important people in your life. Go into the house and bring with you the person you most need to talk with about your future.

Take a few moments to have the conversation you wish to have with this person.

(PAUSE)

When you have finished the conversation, notice how you are feeling about the conversation and this important relationship.

(PAUSE)

Now, clear your screen again. Enjoy the serenity of moving through the sky and taking in the world below.

Turn your attention to the next scene on your bigger-than-life screen. It is two years from now. In the distance you see a woman from behind. She is full of vitality and engrossed in conversation. The woman is talking to a group of people about her work and her dreams and about how she achieved her goals.

As you focus on her, you realize the woman is you, two years from now. You are close enough now to hear her voice. Listen carefully as she describes her work. What is she actually doing? And where? And why does she like it so much? What accomplishments is she especially proud of? How did she achieve her success? How does she feel about her success? How do her family and friends feel about it?

(PAUSE)

Now she has stopped talking and is looking directly at you. You hear her say, "There is one more thing I want you to know that I wish I had known two years ago." You ask her what it is. She leans over and whispers in your ear. . . .

(PAUSE)

What is this important message that she wants you to know? Make a mental note to remember this as you continue your journey into the future.

(PAUSE)

It is now time to begin your descent and prepare for a gentle landing of your magical balloon. As always, you are completely in control of its movement. As you descend, take one last look at the world from this perspective. Enjoy the feelings and sensations of your flight, and know that you can revisit these feelings whenever you choose.

Just ahead is the same clearing where you began your journey. In your absence, a group of people have gathered. As you gently land, the people begin applauding and you realize the applause is for you.

You are being honored with a special award for your special contributions. It may be for contributions in the community, in your career, in your family, or in another important area of your life. Listen closely as the award presentation is being made. Why are you being honored? What have you accomplished that is being recognized by your *community?* How did you accomplish it? How does it feel to have this recognition?

Take pleasure in this and all of your achievements. Let yourself experience the joy and satisfaction you have earned.

(PAUSE)

The celebration is winding down, and now you are ready to leave on the same magical path that brought you here. As you go down the beautiful path, gradually become aware of your present surroundings. Return to your space. Here you will revisit and evaluate the images and experiences of your dream. When you are ready, open your eyes.

(END)

Recording Your Dream Experience

Immediately following the guided imagery, record in detail in your journal everything you remember about what happened: what you saw, heard, and felt in the waking dream. Include things that might seem insignificant to you. Describe your interpretation of the implications of your experience. Use the questions below to jog your memory. However, don't overlook thoughts or feelings that may not fit the questions.

CAN YOU THINK of a word or phrase that captures the essence of your experience?

Describe the physical surroundings of your environment.

YOUR SECRET GARDEN

What was your central life question?

How did your inner guide respond?

Who was the wise old sage? What was in the beautiful box and how is it significant to you?

ANOTHER LIFE FORM

What other life form did you choose to become, and why?

Describe your experience. What one word captures the essence of your experience? How did you feel? What parts of you emerged in this experience?

Describe your reflection in the pond. What insights did you gain about yourself? About your power?

THE HOT-AIR BALLOON RIDE

Describe what you found in the Special Gifts package. What was in the velvet pouch? How did you feel, opening it? How are you using these "gifts" in your life? What happened when you made them the source of power for your balloon?

What did you find in the unlabeled package? What did you choose to throw out of the basket? How did it feel and how did it affect your movement? Did you keep some? If so, what are they and why did you keep them?

THE FUTURE

Describe your experience of being your best self in the different arenas of your life.

Personal: Where were you living? Describe your lifestyle. Who did you bring with you and why? Who did you not bring? Describe the conversation you had with the important person. How did you feel afterwards?

Work: What were you doing? Why did you like it? How did you achieve your success? How did it feel? What did she tell you that she wished she had known two years earlier?

Community/World: Why were you being honored? How did it feel to receive the recognition? What did you do to deserve this recognition?

OVERALL, WHAT WERE your most important learnings from this experience?

Share the Experience

When you have finished recording in your journal, if you have done the exercise with a group, choose a partner with whom you would like to share your experience. Spend about twenty minutes each, sharing and clarifying your most significant insights and discoveries about yourself, your relationships, and your future.

If you did the exercise alone, it is still important to share this experience with another person. My guess is that you'll want to. Tell your "I believe in you" person or your mirror circle. When you tell someone else about your experience, you'll impart even more life to that experience. You'll bring yourself that much closer to making that vision real.

THANKS, MARILYN, for helping us all to see.

You can never outgrow this exercise. It's a way for you to pause and think about your future, fine-tuning the image, that you will find useful over the entire course of your journey to come. Try doing it regularly; you'll find that you get better and better at it. Learn how to see yourself in your future.

Your Dreams, Your Life

I WAS NOT LOOKING FOR MY DREAMS TO INTERPRET MY LIFE, BUT RATHER FOR MY LIFE TO INTERPRET MY DREAMS.

—SUSAN SONTAG

Dreams can be mere wishes (like "I wish I had a million dollars"), or dreams can be vivid pictures and rehearsals of a future in which you can see yourself living happily. Dreams that become so real to your mind's eye that you can almost experience them as reality are dreams that can come true.

> *Life is a self-fulfilling prophecy. Think big, aim high, and the sky is the limit.*
>
> Arlynn Greenbaum, President
> Authors Unlimited

Wishes are energizers. They are fun diversions. But dreams that go beyond wishes have a way of becoming your life.

One of the advertisements for balloon rides in my area proclaims, "Once you have soared above the treetops at sunset, you will never be the same." They are so right.

14

What Do You See When You Close Your Eyes?

WE ALL LIVE IN SUSPENSE, FROM DAY TO DAY, FROM HOUR TO HOUR; IN OTHER WORDS, WE ARE THE HERO OF OUR OWN STORY.

—MARY MCCARTHY

I HAVE A FRIEND, a business owner, who started out in the working world as a journalist. Somewhere along the line, after she'd become a highly successful editor, she decided she needed to "re-pot" herself, as she calls it. So she left her high-powered career. At the age of thirty-two, she went back to get her doctorate in psychology. Now she spends her days in various cities around the world, helping chief executives of all kinds of companies to deal with the personal challenges that come with their positions.

She is able to help these people maximize their potential because she maximized her own. She figured out what her personal definition of success was and then took the steps required to achieve it. She has built her work around her life and her desire to leave a legacy, which is her driving force. Today, she is fully "re-potted," living the life that defines success for *her,* and that is exactly why she is so effective in helping others.

I am in awe of her ability to walk away from hard-won success in one of its many *outward* forms and start anew. To create and achieve her *personal definition of success,* rather than accepting what she had been given or where she ended up. To my mind, she did the near impossible.

I'm not sure which is harder, discovering what you really want out of life or taking the steps to achieve it. I know that doing one without the other doesn't work. With discovery alone, you have nothing more than alternating doses of hope and despair. Joining discovery to action creates fireworks.

A Personal Definition of Success

TO FOLLOW, WITHOUT HALT, ONE AIM: THERE'S THE SECRET OF SUCCESS.

—ANNA PAVLOVA

No one can tell you what the term *success* means to you or should mean to you. There is no universally accepted definition. This is one of those cases in life where whatever you determine to be right for you is right.

You pay for the choice you make, whatever it is. In very real terms, you trade your *life* for the decision you make: the currency is hours, days, and years. It's for keeps. It's forever.

It's a sobering thought, isn't it? Think about it, and you realize the weightiness of this decision that most of us make somewhat haphazardly. At some points in all our lives, we live by the terms and expectations of others. We accept their definitions, the world's definition, of what it means to have a successful life. Now is not one of those times: not now and never again. It's time for you to live for yourself.

Your personal definition of success acts as a magnet in your life, constantly drawing you forward. It provides a feeling of comfort and peace with the decisions you have made about what is important to you. Having that feeling won't eliminate all the pain and suffering. It won't eliminate the trade-offs. I experience it as giving in to the pull of a magnet *inside,* allowing it to show me *which* trade-offs I want to make.

Several years ago, I was participating in a panel discussion at the American College in Bryn Mawr, Pennsylvania. The American College specializes in training insurance executives. One of the instructors was telling me, with both admiration and astonishment, about one of the sales agents who was attending the school.

"One of the best agents I know of," he told me, "is this woman Mary Smith. Boy, can she sell life insurance. Problem is, she only works from nine to three, and then she's off to pick up her kids from school. She makes about $75,000 a year working part-time. If she would just *apply* herself, she could be successful. I don't know what her problem is."

> *Nobody ever said, "Damn, I wish I had led a boring life, worked more, and never gone to Paris."*
>
> Patricia Callahan
>
> Callahan Research

He didn't understand her choices because he was convinced that success was defined 100 percent by how much money you make. But Mary's choice seemed perfect to me. The way she had been able to determine what was important to her and then structure her life in a way that was so obviously different from her peers was inspirational, a sign that it *can* be done.

Finding Your Definition

To discover or clarify your definition of success, begin by recording in your journal the names of five people who *you* think are successful. Who are the five people you most admire for the lives they lead, in whatever respect? Next to each name, describe why you consider that person a success. Is it because of wealth? Nothing necessarily wrong with that; there are no "right" answers to this one. Or is it for some other reason? Is that individual doing something that you wish you could do? What attracts you? What do you see in this person's life that you would like to emulate in some way? As always, be specific. Focus on the details of each one's success definitions, as you see them, that you would like to embrace.

Look at the other side, too. Are there things in their lives that you don't like? What are the trade-offs they've made?

BY ASKING YOU to interpret someone else's definition of success, I'm trying to lead you to create your own *personal* definition. We're so used to observing success in others that we can begin to think it's only other people's definitions of success that count. I want you to reflect on success in other people's lives, but then I want you to switch—permanently—to pursuing *your* vision of a successful life.

This takes time. It's something you'll probably still be working on when we reach the end of this process. But I want you to begin the work now. Very simply, I want you to write a personal definition of success as you see it in this moment.

Here are examples of what three different people wrote:

For me, success is being able to integrate all the parts of my life so that I can be the same person in my work, at home, when I'm making music, whatever. I think each aspect of my life is enriched by being integrated rather than an isolated part of the whole, which has only happened since I left the corporate world and became a consultant.

It keeps changing. When I was in corporate America, I thought it was money and title—and now I just think it's a feeling inside that's peaceful. It's the days I sing in the car on my way home. Actually, I can be more specific. It's having someone to love. It's enjoying what you do. It's having something to dream for.

My personal definition of success is to achieve a seamless flow between independence and interdependence. By independence

> I mean the ability to provide for myself financially, emotionally and physically in order to create a fruitful life. Ironically, it is through independence that I can achieve interdependence. I can extend beyond myself; I can be generous with my time, my money, and most importantly, with my heart and soul. To give is to receive. Thus, independence and interdependence are part of a self-perpetuating cycle that will allow my life to flourish.

But you're looking for the right answer for *you*.

The one limit I would put on you is to ask you to try to avoid pat answers. In every survey I have ever seen, when people are asked what things are most important in their lives, the standard deviation of the responses is almost nil. You can almost predict the most common responses: things like family, career, friends, religion, health, making a contribution.

Those are fine things, important things. They're important to me, too, and I would never suggest that there's anything *wrong* with that kind of answer, except that I notice the way we live our lives often fails to coincide with them. I may say that my health is important and still not manage to give up smoking. I may say that my career is important and still choose not to put in the overtime it would take to get ahead. Whether it's a matter of not being able to make them coincide or not really wanting to makes no difference: the fact is, for most of us, there's almost never a *perfect* fit between what we say is important to us and the way we live our lives.

So let's make *two* lists. First, in your journal, write down a list of the things you think are most important in your life. Then refer back to the matrix you constructed in chapters 6 and 7, and make another list of what your *actions* suggest are the most important things in your life.

I think that, if you're completely honest with yourself, those lists may be different. Look at them: What is the *truth* about what is important to you?

For instance, most of us would probably include "family" in the first list. Yet family doesn't always figure in the actions we choose to take in our daily lives. We often choose working late over spending time with our families. We may think we "have to" put family on that first list, or we may sincerely feel that that *is* what's important to us, but the truth is that many of us do enjoy our work more than we enjoy spending time with our family. That's not always the case, but it is true more times than we will usually admit to ourselves—or to anyone else, for obvious reasons.

I once saw a football coach being interviewed on television. He was asked what the best day in his entire life had been, and he answered: "The day we won the Super Bowl."

"Even better than the day you got married," the reporter continued, "or the day your son was born?"

The coach knew where he was being taken. He said, "Look, I could lie to you, but I'm not going to. The day I won the Super Bowl was the best day of my life. That's the cold, hard truth. It was the best day of my life, hands down."

> *Translate your dreams into realistic goals. Never give up.*
>
> Dr. Maria-Luisa Maccecchini
> President and CEO
> Symphony Pharmaceuticals

My first reaction? "I don't like this guy! I cannot *believe* he would say that!" It offended my sensibilities, challenged my view of what the important things in life were supposed to be. The Super Bowl just wasn't up there on my list!

And that was the problem. *My* list wasn't too important in the *coach's* life. I just thought it should be.

I've changed my opinion of the coach. After thinking about it for days, I realized that one major reason for his success is probably that he has the kind of courage it takes to say what is *really* important to him—no matter what I or anyone else might think—and to follow up with consistent actions.

That's what you should strive for: not necessarily the same goals but the same courage and honesty. You have to be truthful, perhaps to the point of challenging some generally accepted beliefs about what should be important. The honest answer may be jarring, but it is absolutely necessary in order to achieve success in *your* way.

Defining Your Legacy

I THINK THAT PARTLY THE FEAR OF DEATH IS BECAUSE PEOPLE AREN'T READY. THEY HAVEN'T HAD THEIR LIVES.

—MAY SARTON

How would you like people to remember you, once you are gone? What would you like them to say about you when you can no longer hear?

Somewhere buried in your answers to these questions is the essence of what success means to you. Somewhere buried in your thoughts about how you would like to be remembered is your *personal driving force,* the one internal force that is stronger than all the others. It's why you get up in the morning. It's what you are constantly searching for, hoping for. Let's try to find a word that describes that internal force.

To find that one word, I'd like you to write what you hope those closest to you will say when you are gone. If you know what you want them to say, you'll know what you have to do.

When I do this exercise—and I do it at least once a year—it usually starts out with something like "She wasn't afraid to try the untried, and she always gave it her all." I want to be remembered for trying to do things that hadn't been done before. Yet, until I thought about my life in this context, I never realized how important being unafraid was to me.

By doing this you will have a longhand version of your own definition of success. For the shorthand version, pull out a word or two that sums up your driving force. For me, that word is "fearless." What's yours?

With this in hand, you know where you want to go, and how you will recognize your success when you achieve it. You still have time to become the person you want people to remember.

Spinning the Dream

> I LEARNED LONG AGO THAT BEING LEWIS CARROLL IS INFINITELY MORE EXCITING THAN BEING ALICE.
>
> —JOYCE CAROL OATES

Now I want you to look forward in another way. I want you to imagine and describe yourself, in great detail, five years down the road, living your ideal future.

To do this, I'd like you to imagine that you've become so successful in your new life that you're either being profiled in a national magazine or appearing as a guest on a major talk show. You can pick whichever one you're comfortable with; the choice you make could provide you with some clues about yourself. The television interview would emphasize spontaneity and dialogue, while the magazine profile might achieve greater depth.

And remember what I said about making sure your dream should make sense in terms of reality. If your dream is to become the first person to land on Mars . . . well, that's quite a dream, but it's probably not going to happen! On the other hand, this *is* a chance for you to dream big dreams. Don't limit yourself, but explore your dream from a variety of angles, with both enthusiasm and realism.

If you choose the magazine article, pick any magazine you like: a business magazine, a women's magazine, a news magazine, an academic journal, whatever makes sense in terms of your dream. The magazine itself is simply a starting point for the work of your imagination.

And if you've decided you want to write an article for *Fortune*, I still want you to write about what's going on in your personal life and your relationships, as well as in your business. I want you to work in as much detail as you can concerning your new life. What is your work environment like? How do you spend your leisure time? What is your relationship with the people you love? What do your customers or peers say about you? *Why* are you successful?

Take your time with this. Don't try to do it in one sitting. Go over your notes. Talk things over with your mirror circle, your "I believe in you" person, and anyone else you like: ask them where *they* see you, five years down the road. Write a couple of drafts, and as many pages as you want.

If you choose the talk show, pick your favorite. Here's the script: Oprah, Larry King, or someone else has just called and wants to interview you! The host wants you to work with his or her producer to put together a format for your appearance. You're in control.

Now, imagine actually being there, five years from now. See yourself sitting across from the show's host. Here's an opportunity to tell the world what you stand for.

What are you talking about? What are your accomplishments?

Are there any other guests? Who do you want to be there with you?

What's special about what you're doing with your life? Why are you so successful? Why are you so interesting to the millions of viewers?

You are the star of this show. It's a show about what you are living your life for, so use this exercise to pinpoint that. Your purpose will determine what you see in the future and what you make of it. It will drive your real life script.

Now write the scene in your journal, just the way you saw it, heard it, sensed it in your mind. Make it just as real. Add any reflections or feelings you had then or have now.

Don't worry about how well you write. Grades and media critics are not part of the process. This is simply an opportunity to take everything you dream of for the future, imagine it all at once, and then get it down there on paper.

So go ahead now, and give this every ounce of effort and real thought you can.

If it's the right dream for you, seeing yourself living that future will generate excitement and motivation to put the plans in place. That's what we're after, here, because if you can see it, you can be it.

Finally, when you've finished this exercise, I think you should share it with your "I believe in you" person. This experience can be joyous and inspiring for you—I want it to be fun—and sharing it with someone who really cares about your success is a great way of validating the excitement it can bring.

15

Barrier Busting

I HAVE ALWAYS LOVED HORSES. Since childhood, I wanted to own a horse. It took me until I was thirty years old to finally earn enough money to purchase the love of my life, Duke's Dunny, a three-year-old filly. The moment my dream and my reality became one, a funny thing happened to me. I discovered that I was more comfortable with the dreaming part than with the reality.

In my mind's eye, I saw myself galloping through cornfields and meadows, moving swiftly and gracefully, in control and in sync with this powerful and beautiful animal. In reality, all I saw were barriers to why I couldn't do it. First I was just plain scared. By anyone's measurements, these are big animals. My fear led me to construct in my mind all kinds of mental barriers: What if I fall off and get hurt? What if I couldn't go to work? What if the horse goes berserk? What if she doesn't do well in traffic? Maybe I am not a good rider and so on. I had enough excuses to keep me on the ground for almost three months.

I wasn't shy or secretive about my fears and the barriers I felt I needed to overcome. I told anyone and everyone I met what the barriers were to me getting on my horse. I even stood in the stall each night for hours explaining to Duke's Dunny why we were not going out in the woods together. I felt trapped in a dream I could not live.

One night, I was standing in the stall with Duke's Dunny, and the old man who took care of the horses came by for his nightly check. He had seen a lot of horses in his day. He told me what a great horse I had; I launched into my "Yeah, but here are all the reasons I am uncomfortable riding this horse," and he just looked at me and said, "Honey, sometimes you have to just get on your horse and ride!"

The next day I did. And I have been happily doing it ever since. "Get on your horse and ride" has become my battle cry against fears, barriers, problems, and any other such notions that keep my dreams and my reality separate and distinct. Dreams are diversions if you can't meld them into your life, for real.

"Get on your horse and ride" is what we all need to remember, whether our barrier is money, children, lack of education, age, relationships, or our own insecurities. They are all big, overwhelming animals in our minds. *Get on your horse and ride* and take personal responsibility for moving your dream forward.

Barrier busting is a tool and a resource, just like journaling and imaging. The ability to overcome barriers is also a skill, and it takes practice. You learn by doing: you get good at going through barriers by *going through them*. There is no substitute.

"Copies, Please!"

The first time I was forced to think about these issues in a professional context was at the very outset of my career, on my first job, way back in 1976. I was working for a major accounting firm. Women accountants were just beginning to step into the ranks of the "Big Eight" firms, as they were called then.

Looking back, it was really tough. So tough that within a year of our arrival, five of the six other women in my "entering class" at the firm were gone.

I can remember trying to convince that last other woman to stay. I see us riding the elevator up to the sixteenth floor, me begging her not to quit, saying, "It's going to get better! I just know it is!"

I *hoped* it was. But she didn't buy it for a minute. "I didn't go to college," she responded, with the same sadness in her voice that I was feeling, "to spend half of my day xeroxing and the other half being told that I am an idiot." And, very soon thereafter, she was gone.

I didn't have any answer to offer to what she'd said, because there simply wasn't any. We'd each been through too many meetings where a partner would turn to one of us and say, "Would you mind making us fifteen copies of ITT's 10-K report?" And we'd each noticed that we were being asked to do it much more often than the men who'd joined the firm at the same time as us.

If you aren't familiar with 10-Ks, suffice it to say that just one copy can easily require a ream of paper. Get the picture? You definitely weren't going to be back in five minutes. They were paying my salary, though, and if that's what they wanted me to do, how could I argue?

The fact that I would miss most of the meeting, the fact that I didn't see myself as a photocopyist, really didn't matter to anyone but me. I had no choice. So I would smile, pick up the 10-K with both hands, and try my hardest not to let anyone see what was going on inside me.

Yes, I stuck it out. There was nothing I wanted more than to just get away from that kind of treatment, but I stayed put, bit my tongue (often literally), and managed to survive by challenging myself, since it was apparent that no one else was going to challenge me. I would say to myself, "Okay, Rebecca, let's see how fast you can do it. You are not going to miss that meeting!" And I can say with complete confidence that I became the *fastest* 10-K photocopyist in the New York office—meanwhile, putting all of my energy into becoming the best CPA I could be.

I don't mean to overstate what was really a pretty simple, straightforward accomplishment on my part. There are countless people—

including millions of women still facing the same kind of dismissive treatment—who make the same kind of choice I did, every day, day in and day out.

But I don't want to understate the importance of the fundamental *change in thinking* that lay behind my ability to stick it out: I chose what *might be,* rather than what *was,* as the place to invest my energies. Had I not done that, I would never have survived; I would have been forced out the door along with those six other women. Perhaps I would have gone on, as I know they have, to achieve success elsewhere. But the fact remains that I would have been forced to simply run away, and that idea didn't sit very well with me. It still doesn't.

Running Away

Let me be clear about this, though: there's absolutely nothing wrong with wanting to "run away" from something that's keeping you from getting to where you want to go. In a bad situation, it's often the smartest thing to do. What's wrong is taking off before taking the time to identify *exactly* what it is that you want to run away from, and using that knowledge to help determine what you should be heading *toward.* What's wrong is *simply* running away.

I learned back then that I was only going to survive—and, what's more, succeed in bringing about what might be—by articulating to myself exactly what things I hated and then letting go of the hatred. Instead of getting stuck on how much I wanted to run away from being treated like a clerk just because I was a woman, I had to go a step further: I had to understand and accept that *running away, in itself, was only going to get me halfway toward where I wanted to go.*

So let me ask you: Why do you want a change? What are you "running away from?"

I can imagine a lot of people replying to that question, "Everything! The whole kit and caboodle!" I know the feeling. But being able to articulate what it is, specifically, that you want to change in your life is the first step to achieving success. It's what enables you to make sure that the next steps are the right ones.

How can you be sure that the changes you want to effect in your life require a change of place, if you don't know *exactly* what it is about your present situation that you want to get away from? Let me tell you another story.

Carol had spent years in a company she'd given her all to, only to be frustrated in the end because there wasn't any way for her to continue to move up. Switching to another company didn't appear to offer any better prospects, either. So she came to one of our seminars, convinced, almost by default, that business ownership was her only hope.

As she carefully examined her feelings, however, she began to realize that she didn't want to *leave* her company at all. What she really wanted was to have her talents recognized there, to be allowed to use all of them. Her sense of frustration had her convinced that her only choice was to get entirely away from working for someone else; self-examination showed her that there *was* another choice, a better one.

So Carol divorced herself from the feeling that frustration was inevitable as long as she stayed where she was. She divorced herself from the feeling that she couldn't change her situation. And then she did a very courageous thing, an absolute first in her company. She went to her boss and told him that he was in danger of losing a valuable employee. She told him that the company was *going* to give her a leave of absence while she went back to school full-time, and in return, she would come back in two years to revitalize her department.

Well, a few months ago, Carol called to tell me that she'd gotten her master's degree. She was calling from her new office . . . at her old company.

Carol's is a wonderful story of someone identifying her true, specific source of discomfort, and then throwing her energy in *the right direction.* That's what gave her the power to do something unprecedented. She's a great example for all of us.

Until you are able to clearly and confidently articulate what that thing is you want to leave behind, as Carol did, you shouldn't make a move. So I'll ask again: What is it that you want to leave behind? Is it the company you work for? Is it your boss? Is it some aspect of your personal life? Is it something in *you?*

Even those would be too general as answers. Once you verbalize the general problem, then you have to go on to isolate the *specific* problem. Because running away from *everything* leads you to *nothing.*

Never Run from Fear

PEOPLE FAIL FORWARD TO SUCCESS.

—MARY KAY ASH

Figuring out what I wanted to run away from (and understanding why) was the beginning of a lifelong learning process. The lesson (a lesson I find I must continually review) was this: *Barriers have no power over us in and of themselves. We* give them power over us, and *we* must take it back.

> *If you never have any doubts or fear of failure, you should worry!*
>
> Tu-Anh Pham, President
>
> The Virgin Beer Company

Which brings up the biggest barrier of all, the one that can keep us from overcoming any other. Fear.

It's fear that makes us run away *blindly.* When Carol and I were frustrated with our respective situations, we were afraid that we were never going to be allowed to use our talents. But we each came to realize that what we were most afraid of was not being *able* to succeed in changing the situation, not being able to *make* our employers recognize and utilize those talents.

We were afraid of failure, pure and simple, and identifying what it was that we wanted to "run away from" helped us to deal with that fear.

Notice that I said "deal with that fear," not "get rid of it." That's a fear that precious few of us ever leave entirely behind. I think that when someone tells you not to be afraid of failure, they're pretty much asking the impossible.

Abigail Van Buren—"Dear Abby"—was once asked how she achieved her phenomenal success. She answered, "I was not afraid of failing."

Wow, I thought. *How do you get that way?* How do you get to that point in life where you are capable of throwing off everything you've learned since the day you were born and meet the prospect of failure unafraid?

My conclusion? By becoming successful. I would be terribly curious to know if Abigail was saying the same thing before she became "Dear Abby." If so, she's an even more remarkable woman than we already know her to be. As much as I admire her accomplishments, I have to say that success has a way of making the picture we have of our lives a little bit fuzzy.

We are *all* afraid of failure, at least until we can be sure that it'll never happen to us (assuming such a certainty is ever really possible).

So I'm not going to tell you that you have nothing to fear but fear itself. The possibility of failure is *real,* and there is always a price to be paid for failures. To pretend that this reality isn't scary is a big mistake.

It's counterintuitive to try to go in "accepting" the idea of failure. Our minds and our spirits just don't work that way. Our daily experience teaches us just the opposite.

At no point can I remember anyone encouraging me as a kid to be unafraid of failing. As I recall, those who failed were laughed at, set apart, called stupid, discriminated against. You're taught early on to avoid failure at all costs, and they teach the same lesson when you get out in the working world: you learn pretty quickly that no one hires people who fail, no one holds on to people who don't deliver on their promises and hit their targets. Fall short, and you're out of there.

Success gets reinforced with gold stars, A's, and honor roll status; later on, with promotions, titles, and reserved parking spots. If failing were okay, you'd think there would be a couple of tangible rewards for it, wouldn't you? You may say to yourself, "I gained some real wisdom from that failure," but everyone else is saying you screwed up. No, failures are undesirable even if they bring with them all sorts of wisdom.

And then we ask ourselves why we're afraid of failing. Why shouldn't we be?

> *When you wake up in the middle of the night gripped in a cold-sweat fear, your wheels spinning out of control, remember that solutions appear when they're meant to, with or without your help.*
>
> Jessie Close, Restaurateur
> The Leaf & Bean Coffeehouse

But the good news is that fear of failure doesn't have to keep you from achieving success in your life. Fear is a natural part of reaching out to the unknown. It keeps our adrenaline flowing and our antennas tuned in. Fear of failure is bad only if it keeps you from participating fully in the life you have been given because it's *not* trying that's the real killer.

You don't need to become the sort of person who has no fear of failure in order to succeed. Instead, concentrate on being the sort of person who *overcomes barriers.*

You don't need to be fearless to be that sort of person, you need to be persistent. Barriers can be torn down brick by brick, through adopting the right attitude and *taking action.*

Although it may seem like a constant tug-of-war, you can and must find the strength to act and continue to act. Don't give in, even when the odds are stacked against you, and you'll go over any barrier, external or internal.

As you look back a year or two from now, the barriers you've faced will have become a source of satisfying war stories. You'll tell them at dinner parties, to people you meet on the train, to those who are just starting out on a similar path, to anyone who wonders, "How did you do it?" Your stories will be your success history, accounts of an incredible personal journey: *yours.*

"I Choose To!"

EVERYTHING IN LIFE THAT WE REALLY ACCEPT UNDERGOES A CHANGE.

—KATHERINE MANSFIELD

When it comes to taking action to overcome barriers, I think we're always finding new ways of going about it, and continually reshaping and refining the old. Each of us ends up improvising and customizing the tactics to fit our individual situations and capabilities. One of the things I believe this process will achieve is to bring you insights into yourself that will improve your ability to find the tactics that work best for you.

Ultimately, taking action in the world to overcome barriers requires starting with yourself and changing the way you think as well as the way you talk.

I first realized this during the same period I was learning to be a hotshot photocopyist. I was in New York City, living in an "efficiency apartment" (translation: one room), and I had about as much money as I had living space. I was doing some running away, too, at least in my head—still spending more energy in worrying about and talking about my unhappiness than I was in trying to understand it or figuring out what I ought to do if I ever did make a break for it.

Meanwhile, I was on my way to becoming a full-fledged career woman, which meant that I had absolutely *no* free time. On one of the rare Saturdays when I didn't have to work, a friend called and asked me to go with her to a seminar at the New School. Not exactly a seminar, actually: a day-long Gestalt therapy session.

My world at the time was pretty conservatively oriented. I didn't know what Gestalt therapy was. As she told me a bit about it, it sounded fairly exotic, very New York, and definitely not for people who were dressing up in a navy blue suit and red bow tie every day! I've already confessed to you that I haven't always been amenable to "touchy-feely" stuff, and this stuff sounded pretty touchy-feely to me.

But I was going through one of my lonely periods. New York City and fourteen-hour workdays, six or seven days a week, have a way of breeding loneliness. I said, "Sure, I'll come along."

I knew that I wasn't going to get much out of it. What I was secretly hoping for was a chance meeting: that I might find a friend or even a lover. I figured that that made it a pretty good investment of my time.

So I went to a "therapy session" that I knew I couldn't buy into, that wasn't "me" in the least, looking for a relationship. What I found was a new way of thinking that changed my life.

Thirty of us gathered in one of the classrooms, and over the course of this *very* long touchy-feely thing I'd gotten myself into, we did several exercises, all of which were boring me to tears—including one that involved making a list of all the things we "had to do" every day, from the moment we got up in the morning to the moment we shut our eyes at night. And I mean *everything,* big or small, down to unbelievably minor things like "I have to take a shower" and "I have to brush my teeth" and "I have to get dressed" . . . and on and on and on.

When we were done writing our lists, the facilitator told us to lie on our backs on the floor, eyes closed, and listen, as we took turns sharing our lists with the others. Like I said, there were thirty people there. Just imagine lying there listening to:

> I have to take the dog for a walk. I have to take a shower. I have to eat breakfast. I have to get on the subway. I have to go to work. I have to work long hours. I have to pick up the kids. I have to pick up the dry cleaning. I have to prepare dinner. I have to clean my apartment. . . .

This, times thirty! And believe me, what I just gave you was a *very* abbreviated list! I listened to thirty much longer lists of this sort of thing, and it seemed to me that if you'd heard one, you'd heard them all. I read out my own, of course, and it wasn't in the least bit more interesting than anyone else's. I gave up a Saturday for this?

It was one of the longest hours I have ever spent. Here I was, spending a precious day off lying on a dirty floor listening to a detailed account of the drudgery of our collective lives. My hopes of finding a new friend quickly vanished. The only thing I was wishing now was that I hadn't worn my good clothes.

Finally, after all had taken their turns in the spotlight, the facilitator asked us to go back through our lists and change the words "have to" to "choose to." Literally: We were to go through the entire list, meticulously cross out each "have to," and replace it with "choose to." He said he wanted us to experience the difference in feeling that came with the different words.

And then we did it all over again! We followed the same routine as before, taking turns reading our revised lists.

And it *did* feel different. Writing "I have to" had been heavy, tiresome; it weighed on the spirit. Crossing that out and writing "I choose to" had a kick to it! It was energizing, attractive, almost uplifting. And it *sounded* so different, lying there on the same dirty floor listening to those people talking in this strange new way about the most ordinary things.

"But come on," I thought, "we don't have that much choice, in reality. It *feels* better, but it isn't *real*."

I wasn't the only one wondering whether there was any real sense to this. When someone announced that they chose to brush their teeth, one of the other participants said, "Now, wait a minute. You *have* to brush your teeth, don't you?"

"Why?" the instructor countered. "No one is holding a gun to your head each morning and saying that if you don't brush your teeth, you're history! No, we brush each day because we *make that choice*."

I had to admit it made a certain weird sense, if you thought about it that way. And gradually, as the readings continued—"I choose to take the dog for a walk, I choose to take a shower, I choose to eat breakfast . . ."—it started to sink in. As we worked our way back through those thirty lists, stopping here and there to argue the appropriateness of "I choose to," I found it easier and easier to come to the same conclusion: I *do* choose to! *I* am the one making the choices!

I took this new way of thinking home with me, and I can tell you that making this simple change in the way I talked to myself changed my life. It was unsettling, at first. It gave me a feeling I couldn't express, saying "I choose to," while doing things that, deep down, I thought I had to do. But I kept it up and eventually began to call upon an inner strength that gave me the ability to start saying it out loud: "I choose to . . ." And the more I said it, the more real it became.

> *As a girl growing up in suburban America, I was taught that the response "no" means "don't ask again," "never," and/or "case closed." As a woman in America's working environment, I have learned that "no" means "maybe," "present it in a different way," or "come back to me later."*
>
> Deborah Brown
>
> Deborah Brown & Associates

At the same time, the more I said "I choose to," the more I began to question the things I was doing. If I really didn't have to, *why* was I doing them? Some were nothing but habits: I did them because I had always done them, even though I didn't really want to do them. Some seemed to be forced on me . . . but suddenly I wasn't so sure. So gradually, over time, I started to choose *not* to do this or that.

And when it came to things that I didn't want to do but really *did*—at least for the time being—have to do, a subtle yet profound change took place in my thinking. You see, it was this change in language that, as much as anything else, made me begin to understand what was at issue in my desire to run away. It was by examining the various elements of my life and work under the light of "I choose to" that I was able to determine what I *should* run away from and what I should take action to transform.

Something was definitely happening to my attitude. Even better, I began to see that this change in my attitude was bringing results. So I started looking for other ways to change how I thought and spoke.

Where I might have said, "If only I had . . . ," I started to say, *Next time, I will.* Instead of saying, "I really blew it," I tried saying, *I'm one step closer to getting it right.* And I struggled *very* hard to stop saying, "I can't." I turned it around, put it together with "I choose to," and said, *I can do whatever I choose to do.*

It seems like a small enough thing. But every time I spoke to myself or someone else in this new way I was learning, the phrase gave me a feeling of enormous personal power. It literally *breathed life into the future.*

Along the way, I started listening more carefully to the people around me. There were those who were always groaning about what they "had" to do, and those who were apparently *choosing* the way they led their lives. There were those who seemed always to be saying to themselves, "If only . . . ," and those who were *learning* from their "if only's" and eagerly awaiting their next chance. There were those who said it couldn't be done, and those who were *doing it.*

Look around you. You've got the same two kinds of people in your life. Which group is more attractive to you? Which do you prefer to spend your time with? Which is more successful?

Which group do you *choose* to be a part of?

I'm not going to ask you to lie on the floor with your eyes closed. But I *am* going to ask you to make these specific changes in your language and attitude. Your language—along with the attitude it reveals and shapes—can limit you, or it can empower you. *The extent to which you believe in yourself is on display in your language.* Make these small changes in your ways of communicating with yourself and others, and you have the opportunity to make a big impact on your life. It's hard to be a victim when you are communicating *I choose to.*

I want you to take the entirety of your life *in your own two hands,* taking full responsibility for all of the choices you have made and will make in the future. I want you to experience the power you can tap into by internalizing the fact that you don't have to do anything but that you are choosing to do everything you do. The more you do it, the more natural it seems, and the more you take control over your life.

Go Fly a Kite!

Now I've got an exercise for you. I actually want you to go out and fly a kite. When was the last time you did that? Or perhaps just walked around with a big helium balloon?

That long? Well, I think it's about time you did it again.

As soon as you finish reading this chapter, I want you to go out and get a kite or a helium balloon. It's your choice: either one will work for this exercise. First, though, I want you to take a piece of paper and write down just what it is that you *know* you should run away from: just what it is that you're looking to get out of your life forever.

Think as long as you need to in order to come up with the *specific thing* that you are *done with* from this day forward. Write it down on that piece of paper. Write down, too, all the feelings you have and have had about this thing. Your feelings hold your passion and energy, so make sure you dump onto that piece of paper *all* of your feelings about this thing that you're jettisoning from your life. You need every bit of energy you can muster to go from what *is* to what *can be.*

Once you're done, go get that kite or balloon. Roll up the sheet of paper and tie it to the tail of your kite or the string of your balloon. Then go find a big, open field.

Hold those feelings in your hand for a bit, and think about what you're letting go of. If your feelings are tied to a kite, get that kite up in the air, and have some fun sending them this way and that for a while. They're your feelings, and you can do anything you want with them. If they're tied to a helium balloon, just walk around a bit, and feel how they *want* to be released.

Take your time. Enjoy the day. And, when you're good and ready, let them go.

As you watch them fly away, *really let go of them.* Vow to yourself that you are now going to commit *every ounce* of your energy to creating the rest of your life.

Freedom comes when you let go of what has been. Running away only gets you halfway there; letting go and moving forward gets you *all* the way there.

From this moment forward, you're going to concentrate on creating the new. You're going to take action.

16

The Action Plan

WE HAVE REFLECTED, pondered, talked, written, discussed, cried, dreamed, laughed, met, imaged, prepared, felt, played, confronted . . . and changed. From time to time, you may not have seen the point of making all those lists, or doing some of the other exercises I've led you through, but guess what? By going through those exercises, you've made your decision.

Yes, whether you know it or not, you have *already made your decision* about what you want to do with the rest of your life. It's there in the six spheres of your lifescape, in your personal definition of success, in your journal entries, in the way you want to be remembered, and *especially* in the way you described where you want to be five years from now.

I was completely serious when I said, as we started out, that the answers were in you and that I was only going to help you to find them. If you're surprised, if you were expecting a checklist of pros and cons or some formula for calculating the right decision . . . well, I'm sorry. I can't give you one. No one could.

I believe that now, after all the hard work, thought, and feeling you've gone through, you have greater clarity about who you are than you did when we first met. You have a sense of purpose. You know where you must go.

I suspect that you probably stated where you're headed when you "spun a dream" by writing your article or your interview. If you're suddenly thinking, "Wait a minute, I didn't realize you actually expect me to *do* all that!" . . . Yes, I do, if that's what you really *want* to do. I want you to achieve everything you dream of achieving, and I believe that you *can* achieve it.

> *By doing, instead of dreaming and planning, my life has opened into new, exciting directions.*
>
> Frances Wawner
>
> Grandmother and Graduate Student

To fulfill all your hopes for personal success, you need to figure out which steps will take you where you want to go, and then put what's in your heart and mind—your dreams—into action. You are ready to take charge of your life. You have the power to grab the wheel and go in the direction you want, right now. Use it.

Step by Step, from Knowledge to Action

An action plan is like a business plan, in many respects. It is a starting point, not the finish line. It is a dynamic, living, life-oriented document. It's always in the process of being altered, added to, and subtracted from, based on new information obtained, feedback received, lessons learned. Modifications, well-thought-out changes of personal direction, are expected and desirable in response to new situations.

When you've achieved the goals set out in your first plan, it's then time to set new goals, to draw up new plans, to dream new dreams. Let's put your plan together, then, knowing full well that you will keep working on it as you move toward where you want to be.

Your action plan will in fact be made up of six plans, six parts corresponding to the six spheres of life you explored when constructing your lifescape. Each area of your life will be affected in some way by the decisions you make and the actions you take, so you want to be sure to include *all* the aspects of your life in the action plan.

This is where our whole approach, of examining your life in great detail from a variety of angles, bears fruit in terms of concrete, practical steps. Having experienced these six dimensions of yourself, your dreams and goals, and your day-to-day life, you're now equipped with the perspective and the tools necessary to achieve the only kind of success that is truly fulfilling: a *balanced* success, in which each aspect of your life is connected with the others.

The first step is to revisit where you've been over the course of this journey. I'd like you to read through your *entire* journal—yes, all of it!—in order to orient yourself and get ready to use that data while focusing on building your action plan. Look for the interrelationships among your life's six spheres. Look at everything you've written about where you want to be in your ideal future.

Refine your vision and when you've finished going back through your journal, write a few pages that summarize in final form where you are now and what you want from your new life. Include elements that touch upon each part of your lifescape and establish connections.

What you write will be the anchor and reference point for your action plans. As you begin to move forward—and make the inevitable adjustments to those plans—you'll have these pages to look back to, in order to make sure that everything you're doing is designed to direct you toward the large-scale goals you've established.

Finally, looking at each of the six spheres in turn . . .

Resources
Activities
Relationships
Physical Being
Money
Beliefs

. . . you are going to determine the corresponding actions to be taken. Use the following template:

Objectives
Life Factors
Actions Required
Dates Targeted for Completion
Expected Outcomes

As you consider the six spheres in turn, you will probably find that each of them involves more than one Objective. That's fine: one of the main purposes of drawing up action plans is to prioritize; not necessarily to give up any of your Objectives, but to see which are most important to you and therefore know what you should do when.

Similarly, for each Objective, more than one Action and more than one Expected Outcome may be implied. You're likely to find that achieving an Objective in one sphere requires adjusting your Actions—or even your Objectives—in another. Life is never simple; we're each constantly making these sorts of adjustments. Unfortunately, we usually make them on the fly. Your action plans will give you a chance to anticipate problems and conflicts and make your adjustments *before* you're in the thick of things.

Here are the basic steps.

1. Define Your Objectives

Your objectives are, quite simply, what you want to or need to accomplish vis-à-vis one of the spheres of your life. For example, in the relationships sphere, you may be involved in a personal relationship in which you don't find support for what you want to do: your Objective could be to develop that support through communication with the individual involved, or it could be to find the support you need from someone else. In the money sphere, a lack of the funds you need to get to your goal would probably imply Objectives such as earning or borrowing a specific amount.

You need to be quite specific. It's not good enough just to say "I want more support" or "I need more money." You need to define a specific target that you want to hit. "I want to gain support from this person by improving the way we communicate." "I need to earn this much." "I want to borrow this much." In each part of the template, don't settle for anything less than absolute clarity and specificity.

2. Identify the Corresponding Life Factors

Life Factors are the elements, both positive and negative, in your life that have the potential either to hold you back or push you forward as you work toward your specific goal. Take great care in listing them. Go back through your journal and review the information gathered there. Talk with the members of your circle, your support person, and anyone else who might help. Then, identify very precisely the things that will help or hinder you in reaching your objective. For instance, if you want to develop a certain Resource, speak with people who know how that might be done, do research, and then consider the external and internal elements in your life that will have an effect on your ability to do what it takes.

3. Determine the Actions Required

Create actions that increase the effect of the positive Life Factors you've identified and decrease the effect of the negative, always keeping your Objective in mind. A particular Life Factor may require as little as one Action or as many as an entire series of Actions. List all the actions that you must take or think you must take to achieve your Objective. Think through the steps you'll need to take in great detail, and be as specific as you can in laying them out.

4. Set Target Dates for Completion

It's hard to stay on track toward a goal unless you set yourself a timetable. Set a completion date for *each step.*

5. Name Your Expected Outcomes

> *The most important lesson*
> *I have learned is to be myself.*
> *I have to remind myself at times*
> *to call things as I see them,*
> *even if I am nervous about the*
> *imagined consequences.*
>
> Ginny Vanderslice
> Principal Praxis

As you complete each step of the Actions required to reach your Objective, how do you expect the results to move you closer to achieving your personal definition of success? If you have a difficult time relating any Expected Outcome to your larger goals, then an Objective and the Actions required to get you there may not be as important as you thought or may require more clarification. *Don't waste your time working on anything that doesn't really move you closer to your final goal.*

PHEW! WHAT A LOT of work!

Don't worry, you're not supposed to do this in one sitting. You may take several days, even weeks, to get all the data organized and your Objectives and potential Actions clarified.

It's worth the trouble, believe me. It's only by getting a very clear picture of *everything* that you want to accomplish, and how it would be best to go about it, that you're going to be able to set your priorities and move, step by step, toward your ultimate goal.

This isn't just hard work, either; it's a fairly complex process. I think the best way of demonstrating how it's done is to show you a couple of real action plans drawn up by two of the women I've worked with. By studying them, seeing how these women fit actions to objectives across the full range and scope of their lives, you'll be able to discern the thought processes they had to go through.

The two action plans I've picked for illustration are excellent examples of how this tool should be used, and I think you're going to learn a lot from them. The first was drawn up by Margo, who decided at the end of her journey of self-examination that she was going to start a business.

Margo's Action Plan

I'm about to turn 45 and I've decided it's time to take a new journey in my life. I'm ready to be at the helm of my own ship. To the outside world, I am probably the vision of success—but I know that I want more meaning in my whole life, and that includes my work. I want to be more aggressive about what's important to me. I want to bring passion back into my life *and* my work. Having that biopsy recently really helped me get some perspective on my life.

I've devoted the last twenty years to the corporation. I even waited to have a baby until after I hit the senior vice president level. Working 12-hour days, week in and week out, combined with lots of travel and constantly eating out, has really taken its toll on me physically and mentally. I really want not to travel anymore, so I can spend more time with my husband and daughter. I don't want to be out of town again when her next music recital comes along.

I've worked hard to break into the upper echelons of senior management. I love the feeling of accomplishment, but I am ready to be challenged by bigger ideas and to personally profit from my hard work.

Although I'm one of the most respected auditors in the field, I realize that I just don't believe in what I do anymore. It's all been about downsizing and tearing things down. It's for the good of the corporation, but I wonder—for who in the corporation? I want to *build* something permanent, something that leaves a legacy. I want to build something that makes a contribution to other people's lives.

I know I want to—and can—build a business where I feel more in control and where my actions have a positive, lasting effect. I also want to work with a different kind of team—colleagues with no hidden agendas—where the communication is open, and I don't have to leave my heart in the parking lot.

Interestingly enough, one of the things that I am often kidded about is that I am "obsessive-compulsive"—I've been labelled as that by more than one work associate. I like to think of it, though, as great attention to detail and an unending energy to do things right. I actually think that's what made me successful. No matter what I do, I know it's a competitive advantage—and I plan on leveraging that resource to the hilt!

I didn't know where this whole unearthing process would take me, but having worked through it, a lot of the pieces have come together. One of my fondest memories from childhood is from spending time with my grandmother. She was an amazing woman, so full of life, passion, zest. She passed away many years ago—and since I've been so consumed with work, I'd gotten out of touch with my memory of her and the things she taught me. Now I've started thinking again about the way she used to spend her time. She loved music. She was the one who encouraged me to get involved in music—and when I looked at the things I love to do and don't do enough of, it somehow seemed that the most important one was playing music. When I listen to my daughter play the violin, I could almost cry with joy.

Recently, I've been looking at lifecare communities for my mom. She's still living in the same house that I grew up in, but it's just become too burdensome for her to maintain. She's expressed to me that it's time to sell the house and move on to the next phase of her life. It's a big concern to me that she enjoy the last years of her life. Even though she's in her seventies, she's very youthful. So many of the places I looked at were dismal, though. It was very apparent to me what worked and what didn't, and why. Elderly people don't want to stop living just because they're getting older; it's just that their needs have changed. But there aren't any lifecare communities in the towns my mother would like to live in—and there's an enormous need in the surrounding counties here, too!

I'd also like to see a lifecare community where families could come visit and stay a couple of days. I would love my daughter to spend some more time with Mom, but not in an institutional setting.

I could really create something worthwhile here, something that would bridge the generations, and would bring me a great deal of fulfillment. I could create an environment for my mother and others like her to flourish in their golden years—and I'd be thinking of my grandmother too. It would be a tribute to her.

Everything I've read indicates that this is a big industry for the future. I'm ready to take the leap. I want to build a family of lifecare communities, one at a time. That's my move, and I'm willing to take the time to do it right.

I know it won't happen overnight, but I've learned patience over the years. I've certainly got the financial skills and management know-how, but I lack specifics regarding the lifecare industry, and I certainly don't know anything about the health or medical industry. But what I see, what I know in my heart, is that lifecare communities should be about—of all things—life! It's a big dream, no question, but I'm ready to start at the beginning and learn what I need to in order to make this dream a reality. I've definitely got a lot of research and planning to do—but making this decision, and knowing it's the right one for me, feels fantastic. It seems like just reaching this point is really an accomplishment in itself. I feel so energized.

And I'm going to give notice to the company. They've been good to me, and I want to be fair to them. I'm going to try to get a consulting job with some lifecare centers, so I can learn about them from the inside. Maybe I'll meet some prospective partners along the way.

But, whatever happens, my life and I are going to come first, before my business. I heard something on the radio the other day about "re-courtship": falling in love with your husband all over again. I'm ready!

Resources

OBJECTIVES:

To apply my resources to learning about the lifecare industry, with the short-term goal of getting a job or consulting position, and the long-term objective of finding partners and building a family of centers, one by one.

LIFE FACTORS (POSITIVE):

1. I have 20 years of experience, which includes auditing, managing, and finance. I feel very comfortable with the capitalization and financing aspects of building a business, and I'm a very fast learner.
2. I have numerous business contacts that I know how to leverage to my advantage.
3. I am outgoing, diplomatic, and emotionally stable. These aspects, combined with my business background, make me an attractive partner for a venture.
4. I have a passion to leave a legacy. I love old people, like my grandmother. And I want to see my mom happy so I don't have to worry about her.

LIFE FACTORS (NEGATIVE):

1. I have never been a consultant. I've never owned a business or had a business partner (and I know I don't want to do this alone).
2. I don't know anything about the hard parts: the medical implications of running a lifecare community.

ACTIONS REQUIRED (AND TARGET DATES):

1. Keep meeting with my mirror circle. Get their reactions and input regarding my decision and this action plan. (9/1)
2. Give three months' notice to my boss. (9/15)
3. Start doing a lot of research on the industry, including library research and on-site visits (with my mom). Start talking with mom's friends

who have already moved into lifecare communities: see what they like and dislike about where they are. (10/1)

4. Clean up that junk room and start setting up a home office—one that's warm, with plenty of personal photos and an armchair to dream and stargaze in! Order another phone line and get online at home. Post a message through electronic billboards asking for input on medical and other health aspects of my idea. I might get some good leads, plus I can communicate online late at night, which will be helpful with my schedule. (10/15)
5. Contact the consultants I've hired over the years and ask them for advice about setting up as a sole proprietor. Maybe they'll ask me to join them! (11/1)
6. Begin looking for a financial consulting assignment or part-time job at a lifecare center. (11/15)
7. Start developing a preliminary business concept. If I've met potential partners, talk to them about it. (In a year.)
8. Write a business plan. (Two months after I've definitely identified some partners, and we've had a chance to discuss it.)

EXPECTED OUTCOMES:

1. A consulting or part-time job with a lifecare center—the best market research I could conduct!
2. Gathering a talented, well-diversified team to move forward in building and growing the business.
3. A clearer sense of how to integrate my ability to lead a team, my financial expertise, and my desire to build the kind of lifecare communities that I envision.
4. Additional names of individuals I should speak to regarding the medical/health aspects of lifecare communities. My final output from talking to them will be a list of specific risks from that perspective associated with such a venture, and strategies for addressing them.
5. My home office will be a place to collect my research and build a vision for my business.

Activities

OBJECTIVES:

To get a fuller personal life. That means spending more time with my husband, my daughter, and my friends, and also scheduling private time for myself. To get involved with music again; find a group of friends to play with and maybe form a trio. To schedule time to research my business idea. And no more business travel!

LIFE FACTORS (POSITIVE):

1. I yearn for a fuller personal life, and am highly motivated to act on it.
2. The people I want to spend time with have time for me.
3. Once I stop travelling for my company, I'm going to gain the kind of free time I haven't had in years.
4. Before I stopped playing, I used to have quite a talent for the piano and the recorder.

LIFE FACTORS (NEGATIVE):

1. I've almost forgotten what it feels like to do something just for me.
2. Maybe I really *am* a workaholic!
3. Do I have the courage to live my dream?

ACTIONS REQUIRED (AND TARGET DATES):

1. Schedule time in my appointment book for my husband, daughter, and friends. (Start this week.)
2. Find a master class in piano I could attend. (By 10/1.)
3. Make sure I schedule time for the research and other activities I planned in the resource sphere. (Follow resource sphere time line.)

EXPECTED OUTCOMES:

1. I'll find a new pleasure in the days of the week.
2. I'll be a good mom, an accessible wife, and expand my interests.

3. Getting re-involved in music may offer me a new perspective on my life, both professionally and personally. (Maybe I can incorporate music centers into the lifecare communities?)

Physical Being

Objectives:

Rejuvenate myself physically, since I have neglected myself so badly in the last few years. I really need time to clear my thinking and get back in touch with my body. Now that my daughter is older, we can exercise together. Decompress from corporate life.

Life Factors (Positive):

1. I'm at the mid-point in my life and the positive changes I make in the way I treat myself will contribute to my vitality as I go forward.
2. When I make something a priority, I do it!
3. Three months is soon!

Life Factors (Negative):

1. I still have obligations in my current job that will make it difficult for me to initiate this change right away.
2. The doctor said that I should remember there has been a lot of cancer in my family.
3. I can't stand looking at myself naked in the mirror.

Actions Required (and Target Dates):

1. Research the family membership plans available in the health clubs in our area. (This week.)
2. Plan a getaway alone with my husband after my last week of work. Call my brother to see if we could use his beach house for a few weeks. (By 9/15.)
3. Schedule a doctor's appointment for another mammogram. (By 12/15.)

EXPECTED OUTCOMES:

1. I'll feel less stressed.
2. I'll have fun exercising with my daughter.
3. I'll be able to feel comfortable again in a bathing suit.

RELATIONSHIPS

OBJECTIVES:

Focus on the people I love and who love me. Be fully present with them. Rekindle some old friendships with women friends. Spend some time with my mom visiting lifecare centers, and listening more to her dreams about the rest of her life.

LIFE FACTORS (POSITIVE):

1. I have a wonderful daughter and husband who love me.
2. I have some friendships that go back to childhood.
3. My mom is physically active, healthy, and can drive her own car.
4. My husband believes in me and my new business idea.
5. My daughter is excited about my home office. She asked if she could start a business there too!

LIFE FACTORS (NEGATIVE):

1. My daughter is growing so fast. I don't want to miss her childhood!
2. Whenever I'm with my husband on the weekend, I'm exhausted from all the travelling.
3. My mom is really critical, and has no trouble telling me what a bad mom and wife I am.
4. Being an only child puts a lot of pressure and guilt on me. I feel like I am her parent now.
5. A lot of my old school buddies live far away.

ACTIONS REQUIRED (AND TARGET DATES):

1. Schedule time with my daughter to visit the health clubs. Value her input. (This week.)
2. Plan a family vacation for after Christmas. And promise them: no phone calls, no faxes, and I'm going to stay the whole time. (By 12/1.)
3. Pick up the phone and call my old buddies. Tell them the good news! (This weekend.)
4. Schedule time with mom to visit some lifecare centers. Tell her about my dreams to build lifecare centers and tell her how much I would value her ideas and dreams. Get her to talk to her buddies, too. (10/1)

EXPECTED OUTCOMES:

1. A richer, more rewarding personal life because I will have meaning in my life.
2. Less guilt and remorse about my life.
3. A greater sense of connection to the world through my relationships and my work.

MONEY

OBJECTIVES:

A clear and comprehensive picture of my financial future. I need to thoroughly assess how much money we need to live on, re-do my household budgets, figure out what kind of salary I need in my consulting work. I need to dramatically reduce cash outlays. I also need to talk with my mom about her financial picture.

LIFE FACTORS (POSITIVE):

1. I have built up a solid pension and I am willing to take some short-term financial risks in order to create the life I want.
2. My husband wants to be married to a person who loves what she does, and supports my business vision. Since I put him through graduate school, he'll help me through.

3. I am confident that if there is a way to build a profitable lifecare business, I can do it.

LIFE FACTORS (NEGATIVE):

1. I am nervous about not having a paycheck for a while. I know that I can live with that. I've thought long and hard about it. Nonetheless, it is scary.
2. I have expensive tastes. I'm used to wearing expensive clothing. It will be a major lifestyle change for me not to have a lot of excess disposable income.
3. I've never been a consultant or a business owner.

ACTIONS REQUIRED (AND TARGET DATES):

1. Contact the benefits office of my company. Find out the premiums I need to pay for health insurance, once I leave. Get specific information on the payout of my pension and the impending penalties I will face for early withdrawal. (Week of 9/15.)
2. Determine a personal monthly household budget for when I leave my job. Examine different scenarios from best case to worst case to share with my husband. (By 11/15.)
3. Talk with mom about her financial picture. I know this is going to be awkward, but it's important. I don't think she has enough money to live comfortably for the rest of her life. (By 11/1.)
4. Get more information about what kinds of fees consultants are getting these days. (11/1)

EXPECTED OUTCOMES:

1. A financial plan for the next three years based on the different scenarios.
2. A feeling of control because I will have learned more about my mom's financial picture, so that I can begin to manage her money more effectively and know whether or not I will be supporting her.
3. A different kind of security based on doing what I love to do, instead of what the numbers say.

4. Detailed information regarding what kinds of consulting fees I can realistically charge.
5. A clear understanding of my health and pension benefits that I can utilize in formulating my new budget.

BELIEFS

OBJECTIVES:

I want my work to be involved in creating things, not downsizing and reorganizing. It's important to me that I leave a legacy and work at something that builds better lives for people. I want there to be passion in my life for what I do.

LIFE FACTORS (POSITIVE):

1. I'm ready to make a change.
2. This feels right.

LIFE FACTORS (NEGATIVE):

1. Right now, I feel really worn down physically and mentally.
2. This is the biggest change I've ever tried to implement in my life.
3. I'm scared that my ambitions are too lofty.

ACTIONS REQUIRED:

1. Write in my journal every week to stay in touch with my innermost self and what's important.
2. Spend more time thinking and dreaming. Take a long walk by myself early Sunday mornings, before everyone wakes up.

EXPECTED OUTCOMES:

1. A person who is more at peace with the choices she has made about her life.
2. A person who smiles a lot more.

YOU CAN SEE that Margo is trying to look from every angle at the consequences of her decision to start a business—and that kind of planning greatly increases her chances for success. Now, here's an action plan from someone who decided that she wasn't going to start a business . . . at least, not right away.

Nicole's Action Plan

I've just turned thirty and feel like I have a lot of things to balance in my life. Being newly married, it's important to me that Jack and I take time to build a strong foundation for our marriage. We're both still paying off debt from graduate school, and we'd like to start a family. There's so much to consider. When I think about what I want my life to look like in five years, I know I want a solid, happy marriage, a child, and work that I really enjoy.

I feel like there are a lot of valuable ways for me to spend my professional time. My most important priority is to make my corporate career work effectively. I think I gain a lot from being employed where I am, and that the company gets a lot of value from me as an employee. Since I want to focus on my marriage, and I know that Jack and I want to have a child in the next two or three years, I don't realistically think that business ownership is viable right now. I'd like to reconsider it as an option, however, in the next five or six years. In the meantime, the security of working for the corporation, the opportunity to build my pension, and the ability to have a fixed maternity leave are all extremely attractive. I'm not ready to give those up in light of my desire to have a family.

Unfortunately, my current position in the company is not as rewarding as I would like. I really enjoyed being in the manufacturing area of my company, where I could use my strengths and experience. I need to feel valuable and know that each day I am making a contribution. Now that I've been moved to marketing, that's not the case. I'm starting all over and I don't have the opportunity to make a significant impact. I miss that.

My priorities right now are to try and make my current marketing assignment more enjoyable and rewarding. Marketing is a very valued function in this company, and to the extent that I do well here, I could advance my career significantly. However, I want to maintain my contacts in manufacturing. It may be that I can be most effective in that function, and that the only way for me to lead a balanced life is to move back into that area. As a much more distant option—in the next five to six years—I want to position myself to be able to use my background in manufacturing to do consulting on my own. I think I can use the time I'm spending in marketing as a tool for selling my abilities as a consultant, because there are so few manufacturing people who can relate effectively with people in marketing and vice versa. I think this could be a real competitive advantage for me, whether I stay with the company or go out on my own.

I want to manage my career so that I have options that can accommodate my desires to lead a fulfilling personal life. I know that I could never stop working when I have a family, because making a contribution through work is important to my self-esteem and because I need to feel that I'm making a financial contribution to my marriage. I'm uncomfortable with the idea of not having work as an integral part of my life, even when I do have children.

RESOURCES

RESOURCES OBJECTIVE #1:

I want to use my skills and talents in a way that makes me feel like I'm making a contribution to the corporation, but that also allows me to have a balanced life.

LIFE FACTORS (POSITIVE):

1. I have already experienced a better work-life balance, when I was working in the manufacturing area of the company.
2. I had a strong reputation in manufacturing for delivering results. My performance reviews have been outstanding, and I therefore have a very strong track record with the company.
3. I have good contacts with people higher up in the company who value

my skills and education and want me to succeed and stay with the company.

4. My husband is supportive when it comes to temporary work/home life imbalances. He'll take charge of chores if I have to work late.

LIFE FACTORS (NEGATIVE):

1. The people here in marketing don't seem to place the same value on balance as we did back in manufacturing.
2. My new boss doesn't really have a life outside of work. He works very lengthy hours, has no significant other, generates work that is very often needless or not well-thought-out, and values spending long hours in the office (known around here as "face time"), not performance.
3. I have difficulty not conforming to corporate culture expectations as they are exemplified within a department.
4. My husband will not tolerate long-term work/home life imbalances.

ACTIONS REQUIRED (AND TARGET DATES):

1. Discuss the demands and culture of my current work environment with my husband. (Next two weeks.)
2. Establish a schedule for communicating and maintaining my relationships with contacts in the manufacturing department, in the event that I decide it would be appropriate to move back into that department. (Set up one contact lunch per month. Make one phone call every two weeks.)
3. Determine the best way to approach my current boss about establishing definitive work hours, and then initiate the conversation. (Within the next quarter.)
4. Contact and maintain communication with higher-ups in the company who value my education, experience, and reputation, so that I'm not dependent on my current boss for future career opportunities. (Schedule one lunch per quarter.)
5. Determine ways that I can influence my current work group so that we can work smarter as a team as well as individually. (Identify ways

within next two weeks. Implementation will require constant example and possible discussion will be ongoing.)

EXPECTED OUTCOMES:

1. A strong reputation within the corporation and respect for my performance.
2. A network of career contacts that will produce new opportunities in the future.
3. Resistance from my current boss over his expectations regarding face time versus performance.
4. A not-so-balanced personal life in the short term, but a higher chance of a balanced personal life in the future.
5. Improved working environment and attitude within my team.

RESOURCES OBJECTIVE #2:

Develop a broad understanding of marketing in the short term, so that I can improve my skills in communicating between different functional areas within the corporation.

LIFE FACTORS (POSITIVE):

1. I am currently positioned to develop a broad understanding of this functional area.
2. I am a quick study.
3. My understanding of manufacturing makes me more effective in this new area, because I bring to light consequences of business decisions that my peers do not understand.
4. I have significant time in and exposure to the company, which greatly helps me to see patterns and trends within the business and its industry.

LIFE FACTORS (NEGATIVE):

1. I don't like the culture in the marketing department.
2. Working in marketing will create imbalance in my personal life.

3. I don't have a great deal of decision-making responsibility in the marketing department, since I'm at the bottom of the totem pole.

ACTIONS REQUIRED (AND TARGET DATES):

1. Establish a time-frame with my boss regarding the length of this marketing assignment. I would like to move up and gain more responsibility before I totally eliminate marketing as a career option. (Within the quarter.)
2. Schedule lunch on a regular basis with marketing peers I respect, to maximize my breadth of understanding about the function while I'm involved with this department. (One lunch per month.)
3. Keep a work journal which documents the connections between marketing and manufacturing. Use this as a tool for developing future consulting ideas. (Make an entry every Friday before I leave work.)

EXPECTED OUTCOMES:

1. A solid breadth of understanding about the marketing function.
2. An understanding of the conflicts and management problems that arise between marketing and manufacturing, and of strategies for mitigating and overcoming such obstacles.
3. A better understanding of how to position myself as a future consultant.

ACTIVITIES

ACTIVITIES OBJECTIVE #1:

Minimize the amount of time I spend each week on domestic chores.

LIFE FACTORS (POSITIVE):

1. Jack doesn't expect me to cook dinner every night. He will make dinner if he has time, or we'll pick something up.
2. We live in a small apartment, so there isn't an extensive amount of maintenance needed on a daily basis.

LIFE FACTORS (NEGATIVE):

1. The cats shed a lot. We need to keep on top of vacuuming and dusting because of them.
2. I'm afraid I'll gain weight if we keep eating Chinese take-out twice a week!

ACTIONS REQUIRED (AND TARGET DATES):

1. Review with Jack how we can work a cleaning service into our budget once every two weeks. (Within the week.)
2. Talk with neighbors about who cleans their apartments. Check around for other recommendations. Contact a highly recommended cleaning service and set up a schedule. (Within the month.)
3. Investigate health food take-out places that are close to the apartment. Discuss with Jack the fact that I'd like to cut back on greasy foods on the nights we order out or pick up. (Within the month.)

EXPECTED OUTCOMES:

1. More time to spend with Jack in the evenings and on the weekends.
2. Less stress about having too little time.

PHYSICAL BEING

PHYSICAL OBJECTIVE #1:

Since I'm a morning person, I want to rearrange my days so that I can accomplish more at work in the early part of the day and do less intellectually demanding tasks in the later part of the day.

LIFE FACTORS (POSITIVE):

1. Most departmental meetings are scheduled later in the day, which frees up my mornings for intensive individual work.
2. I can accomplish more by 9:00 A.M. than most people do all day!

LIFE FACTORS (NEGATIVE):

1. My boss doesn't come in until 9:30 A.M. and stays until 10:00 P.M. He doesn't realize that I am often in by 6:30 A.M., so that my leaving by 6:00 P.M. doesn't mean I'm short-changing the company.

ACTIONS REQUIRED (AND TARGET DATES):

1. Talk with my boss about my hours and his expectations regarding performance versus face time. (Within the quarter.)
2. Make a personal commitment to myself not to be rattled by peer pressure or comments regarding the face time I put in, when I am meeting and exceeding performance requirements. (Continuous. Write about this in journal once a week, to vent frustrations and work out mental conflicts.)

EXPECTED OUTCOMES:

1. To the extent possible, a better balance between work and home life in the short term.
2. More time available in the evenings to spend with my husband.

PHYSICAL OBJECTIVE #2:

I want to maintain an exercise program that doesn't conflict with time I want and need to spend with Jack.

LIFE FACTORS (POSITIVE):

1. Exercise gives me more energy to get things accomplished and keeps me sane!
2. I'm already in decent shape and don't have to invest a lot of time to get there—just enough to maintain it.

LIFE FACTORS (NEGATIVE):

1. Jack likes to work out in the morning. I prefer to work out in the evening.
2. Jack gets upset if I choose an aerobics class over him.

ACTIONS REQUIRED (AND TARGET DATES):

1. Talk with Jack about how we can find time to exercise together. Maybe we can just do it once a week, if he wants to keep working out in the morning. Or we could plan outings on the weekend that are more athletic in nature. (This week.)
2. Investigate gyms that are closer to work. (Within the month.)

EXPECTED OUTCOMES:

1. Better communication between my husband and me regarding expectations on how and when we spend time together.
2. Good health and less stress!

Relationships

RELATIONSHIPS OBJECTIVE #1:

I want to spend as much quality time together with Jack as possible. I really believe that it is important to build and strengthen the foundation of our marriage before we have a child.

LIFE FACTORS (POSITIVE):

1. Jack and I are very much in love and value our commitment to each other.
2. Jack and I both agree that we want to establish our careers and our marriage before we have children.

LIFE FACTORS (NEGATIVE):

1. There is so little time, and just not enough to do everything! As a two-career couple, it's hard to carve out quality time for the two of us alone.

ACTIONS REQUIRED (AND TARGET DATES):

1. Schedule a long weekend away once a quarter where Jack and I can concentrate on each other. (Schedule first one within the next three months.)

2. Set aside one night a week as a "date night," so that neither of us makes any conflicting plans. (NOW.)

EXPECTED OUTCOMES:

1. More quality time with Jack so that we can discuss our priorities and long-term plans with each other.
2. Improved intimacy between us and more "down-time" to maintain a sense of fun in our lives.
3. This will help to prepare us for moving to the next phase of our marriage: children.

RELATIONSHIPS OBJECTIVE #2:

Now that I'm not living near my mother anymore, I'm always feeling guilty about not being there for her. I need to eliminate the feelings of guilt I have around my relationship with her.

LIFE FACTORS (POSITIVE):

1. I want and need to have my mother in my life.
2. My mother and I get along much better now that I'm married and live in another state.

LIFE FACTORS (NEGATIVE):

1. My mother doesn't understand my desire to have a career and a family.

ACTIONS REQUIRED (AND TARGET DATES):

1. Schedule a weekly phone call with my mother so that she doesn't nag me about calling, and so she has something to look forward to that she can count on. (Talk about it this week.)
2. Write in my journal about my frustrations rather than allowing myself to stew over them. I need to discharge the negative feelings and then move on. (NOW.)

EXPECTED OUTCOMES:

1. Less nagging from my mom.
2. I will be more relaxed because I won't be internalizing my guilt.

RELATIONSHIPS OBJECTIVE #3:

Jack and I really want to start having a family within the next two or three years.

LIFE FACTORS (POSITIVE):

1. I'm young, healthy, and have plenty of time to have a child.
2. Jack and I agree that we want to pay off our educational debt before we have children.

LIFE FACTORS (NEGATIVE):

1. I'm not sure how I will integrate work with having a baby.

ACTIONS REQUIRED (AND TARGET DATES):

1. Look into maternity leave at the corporation. (Within the next six months.)
2. Talk with other working moms at the corporation. (Within the next six months.)
3. Talk to three working moms who have consulting businesses, to determine whether that might be a feasible option for me in the future. (Within the next six months.)

EXPECTED OUTCOMES:

1. Additional questions and details that I can use to continue investigating options surrounding pregnancy and work.
2. A better understanding of how I can approach integrating my desire to have a family and still be involved in meaningful work outside the home.

MONEY

MONEY OBJECTIVE #1:

I would like to pay off my education debt before I have a child.

LIFE FACTORS (POSITIVE):

1. My raises at work have been steady and consistent.
2. I only have three years to go! (Or is that a negative?)

LIFE FACTORS (NEGATIVE):

1. I'd like to accelerate my payment schedule, but don't think I can afford it.
2. I have a large balloon payment at the end of the last year.

ACTIONS REQUIRED (AND TARGET DATES):

1. Go over the budget with a fine-tooth comb with Jack and figure out if there are any places where we're both willing to sacrifice in order to speed up the payment schedule. (Within the next two months.)
2. Determine if my projected pay raises will cover the balloon payment at the end of the last year, so that I don't have to take money out of savings to meet it. Earmark that money now for that purpose! (Within the next two months.)

EXPECTED OUTCOMES:

1. Peace of mind!
2. Money available to handle childcare expenses.

MONEY OBJECTIVE #2:

I want to explore financing needs for starting my own consulting business sometime in the future.

LIFE FACTORS (POSITIVE):

1. I have the freedom now to investigate this option thoroughly, before committing to it. The steps I take now will give me more flexibility in the future.
2. I have an excellent credit history, which should enable me to obtain a loan.

LIFE FACTORS (NEGATIVE):

1. I won't use personal collateral to secure a loan once I have a child.

ACTIONS REQUIRED (AND TARGET DATES):

1. Determine through research how much I would need to start a consulting business. (Within the next six months.)
2. Research options for financing a business, once I determine how much money I would need. Find out the criteria I would need to meet in order to get a loan. By getting my "ducks in a row" now, I'll be better able to make this a viable option in the future. (Within the next six months.)

EXPECTED OUTCOMES:

1. More insight into what it takes to get a business off the ground, from a financing perspective.
2. Better understanding of lending criteria.

MONEY OBJECTIVE #3:

Jack and I want to buy a residential property before we have children.

LIFE FACTORS (POSITIVE):

1. We've been setting aside money for a down payment on a regular basis.
2. We both view this as a high priority.

LIFE FACTORS (NEGATIVE):

1. We can't agree on where we want to buy.
2. We might have difficulty maintaining a mortgage payment in the future if I start a business and my income is unpredictable.

ACTIONS REQUIRED (AND TARGET DATES):

1. Make a list with Jack of all the areas we each would like to live in, and start to visit them. Be open to everything in the beginning and see what we like. (Within the year.)
2. Figure out how much mortgage we can afford, with and without my salary. (Within the year.)
3. Discuss issues which require compromise and determine how we will resolve them. (Within the year.)

EXPECTED OUTCOMES:

1. A plan for moving forward on purchasing a home.
2. Creative brainstorming sessions on how to meet our goals as a family.

BELIEFS

OBJECTIVE:

I want my life to be filled with beauty, excellence, love, laughter, and companionship. Those aspects are the most important ones to me in living a daily life that is meaningful.

LIFE FACTORS (POSITIVE):

1. Identifying the things that make me happy means that I can choose to seek out those things in my life.

LIFE FACTORS (NEGATIVE):

1. Sometimes it seems so hard to keep the responsibilities of daily living from overwhelming me, and I can lose sight of the things that are most important to me.

ACTIONS REQUIRED (AND TARGET DATES):

1. I will commit fifteen minutes a day for quiet time, solely for the purposes of reconnecting with my key beliefs and reminding myself why I undertake the activities that I do during the day. (Now and continuing forward.)

EXPECTED OUTCOME:

A happy, balanced life that I love!

YOU'RE PROBABLY going to have more than one Objective in mind for each sphere, as did Nicole. Like her, you'll need to prioritize, weighing each Objective in terms of your ultimate goal and the most advisable way of getting there. Of course, it's still necessary for you to consider *all* the spheres, in order to avoid having actions in one sphere interfere with actions in another, and you may need to make adjustments. Even though the actual process of completing this step may be complex, the principle is fairly simple: determining which one of the Objectives in each sphere is Priority One, at least for now.

I can't lead you through this step, because it's completely tied to the particulars of your life and your goals. There are three questions, though, that I'd suggest you ask yourself in setting your priorities:

1. Which of these Objectives makes the most sense as a first step, in terms of reaching my ultimate goal?
2. Which of these Objectives, when I reach it, is going to provide me with the greatest sense of fulfillment, energy, momentum, and direction, as I move on to other Objectives?

3. Which of these Objectives is most in line with my need to marshall support from the other people in my life and my desire to accommodate their needs?

Your answers to these three questions are not necessarily going to be identical. If they are, you're very lucky, and in good shape to move ahead. Usually, though, there are trade-offs involved in becoming who you want to be. Only you can weigh all the factors and decide upon the trade-offs you're going to have to make—or are willing to make.

If something isn't critical, if it doesn't seriously affect the outcome, then don't worry about it. But if something *is* critical—an objective, a personal concern, a consideration in the interest of others—then don't give it short shrift. Focus on the things that will truly make a difference and that are truly important to you.

Now It's Your Turn

So sit down now and start sorting through your Objectives and drawing up your action plans. Once you've determined what your first set of plans are going to be, you'll be prepared to ensure that no aspect of your life is ignored as you begin to turn your dreams into reality.

I've done this myself, and I know just how exciting a moment it is, how good it feels after all that hard work, to see just what it is I'm going to do in order to become the person I want to be. I've been with other people as they came to the same point, and it's a fantastic moment to share in.

Although I can't be there as you arrive at your action plan, as someone who's been through the process, I am certainly with you in spirit.

Speaking of spirit, I want to add one more thing to your to-do list. Now that you've completed your action plan, but before you do anything else, I want you to gather together as many of the people whom you've turned to in the course of this journey as you can, and celebrate the spirit of this occasion! I want you to celebrate *your* spirit and the spirit of helpfulness and caring that brought you all together.

> *Success isn't a dot at the end of the road map. It's more like a series of doors to open.*
>
> Georgette Mosbacher, President
> Georgette Mosbacher Enterprises

You've got a lot of work ahead of you, and I know you can do it. Through it all, always, always, remember to celebrate. Mark the small successes and the big ones. Above all, keep doing what you love, and every day will be a celebration.

Congratulations!

CONCLUSION

The Road Ahead

I THINK MOST OF us carry around in our heads an image of ourselves in the future. We see ourselves accomplishing something, living out one of our dreams, changing and growing, being in a place of our choosing.

The image I carried around in my head for years was taken from, of all places, a TV commercial for Apple Computers that ran several years ago. The scene takes place at night. A young man is riding his bicycle through what looks like the deserted streets of the Wall Street area of New York City. He is riding with purpose; you can see that he knows where he is going, what he wants to do. His golden retriever is running along beside him.

Then the commercial cuts to a shot of the man in his large but very personal office. He's working at his computer; you can hear the click of each keystroke. The camera pans across the room. You see the bicycle propped up against the wall, the dog curled up at his feet.

That image stuck with me. It was an image of the working world I wanted but, up to that point, had never articulated.

"That's what I want to do when I grow up," I thought. I wanted to have Charlie, my Old English sheepdog, best friend, and constant companion, with me at the office too! I wanted to do my work when I was at my best. I wanted to work with people I respected and liked. I wanted to integrate all the parts of my life. I wanted permission to be me, and in a strange way that commercial gave me the wake-up call I needed.

Capital Rose's home is now a meticulously renovated nineteenth-century building located in the heart of Chester County, Pennsylvania. To one side of the building is a 250-acre working farm; to the other, a digital computer-imaging business. It's a place of old and new, of change and security, of tradition and dreams. It's the perfect place for fostering innovation and creativity. It's the place for me.

Somehow, it has all come together in a place that reflects the life I choose to lead. I knew I wanted to be in a place like this long before I found it. The journey to get here was long and trying at times, but I'm here now. I'm here working early in the morning. I'm here late at night. I feel as though I was meant to end up here.

And, yes, Charlie loves it too. He has kept a constant vigil under my desk throughout the course of writing this book. Without knowing it, he has become the sign of my fulfillment, of the fact that I am living the kind of life I want to live. It's nice, feeling that I'm where I belong. It's even nicer having Charlie here with me.

There was a time when I thought it would just happen. "Someday," I told myself, "I'm going to be able to bring Charlie to the office, just like that guy in the commercial. I don't know how, I don't know when, but someday it's going to happen." Yes, I'm an optimist, a true believer in dreams coming true. I think every one of us has the right to dream big dreams.

But our dreams must be backed up with one thing: lots of really hard work. Usually, years of hard work. In my experience, the overnight success stories generally turn out to have taken five or ten years to achieve.

Dreams don't just come true. Being what we want to be and doing what we want to do with our lives don't just happen. Dreams are made real one step at a time, over the proverbial long haul. Dreams take long-term commitment. From first to last, we need focus, discipline, persistence, and the ability to keep in sight the vision of what we are slowly creating.

Over the past several years I have been continuously surprised by the number of women I've met—ordinary women like you and me, like my mother and your mother—who are doing extraordinary things with and in their lives. I've become convinced that each one of us has a special something deep inside of us, waiting to be expressed, waiting to lead us on to success and happiness. We may not know exactly what it is yet, but there's no doubt that it's there.

My wish for you is that you bring into reality the most heartfelt image of success that you carry within you, and that you continue to seek and find in yourself that special gift only you have been given. Once you find it, share it with those around you, and work together with them to bring your dream to life.

Oliver Wendell Holmes once said, "Most people go to the grave with their music still inside them." Only you can make sure that that doesn't happen to you.

My best to you.

ACKNOWLEDGMENTS

NO ONE DOES IT ALONE, and I didn't either.

The credit for guiding this book from concept to publication goes unreservedly to my business partner and good friend Alina Wheeler. She was with me through the entire process, cheering me on, challenging me, and motivating me to push harder toward clarity and meaning.

To my "I believe in you" group: Carol Novello, Jean Brooks, Heather Norcini, Marilyn Sifford, Marjorie Gorman, Karol Wasylyshyn, Virginia Vanderslice, Patricia Remeis, Emmy Remeis, and Richard Cress: I thank you from the bottom of my heart for caring enough about me to invest your time, intelligence, soul, and energy in this project.

To my agents, Ling Lucas and Ed Vesneske, Jr., of Nine Muses and Apollo, thanks for finding me and convincing me to write this book. But most of all I want to thank you for going well beyond the call of duty. You have been so much more than my agents over the past two years; you have been my friends, the voices I turned to when the going got tough. I will never be able to thank you enough for understanding the power of the work we are doing at Capital Rose and enabling me to share it with so many people.

I want to thank Mindy Werner, senior editor at Viking Penguin: Your fellow editors advised me early on that you know how to make a book. Your counsel on the structure of the book was invaluable.

I want to thank Sue Hunnicutt, vice president, and Tim Feige, senior vice president, of The Prudential. You were the first individuals within Corporate America to risk believing in our mission and supporting us with resources and wisdom. There is something very special and very hard about being first.

I have been extremely fortunate to work with a group of individuals who are risk takers and visionaries. We hear about the dearth of leaders within our corporations, but they are there; our challenge is to hear them. I want to thank Cindy Sobieski and Bill Lutz with Deloitte & Touche, and Peter Rohr and Barry Gross with Merrill Lynch, for your words, your actions, and your support.

To all the women business owners and women who want to be business owners with whom I have had the privilege to work over the last five years, I thank you for sharing with me and teaching me what it's all about. Many of you are represented in this book through your insights and quotes. Mentoring takes many forms; you have provided wisdom and counsel for those who must face decisions you have already encountered. May we all continue to be there, sharing, with those who want our guidance and encouragement.

And finally, I would like to thank my dogs, Marigold, Charlie, Lisa Jane, and Susie, for being my constant companions throughout the writing process and in my life.

FROM CAPITAL ROSE, INC.

Inc. Your Dreams, audiotapes
Listen to these tapes in the car or use them as a companion for doing the exercises within the book. Read by Rebecca Maddox. Abridged; three hours on two audiocassettes, $16.95.

When Was the Last Time Someone Said I Believe in You, audiotape, with an introduction by Debbi Fields of Mrs. Fields Cookies
"I believe in you" are the four most powerful words that we can say to one another. Hearing those words can unleash our potential. Take this opportunity to reaffirm your belief in yourself—or someone else—and listen to the inspirational words of Rebecca Maddox as she talks about the importance of people helping one another succeed. One audiocassette, $9.95.

To order, please call (610) 644-4212. Prices do not include shipping, handling, or taxes.

Contact us if you'd like to know about seminars or presentations in your area, or about other publications or products from Capital Rose. We'd be happy to hear from you.

Capital Rose, Inc.
690 Sugartown Road
Malvern, PA 19355

Information on The Capital Rose Perpetual Fund

The Capital Rose Perpetual Fund is an unprecedented enterprise to build a $40 million fund to finance women-owned businesses through a national, grassroots effort to raise individual contributions of $10 from four million women and men. Please call or write to find out how you can become a part of this ground-breaking initiative.

FOR THE BEST IN PAPERBACKS, LOOK FOR THE 

In every corner of the world, on every subject under the sun, Penguin represents quality and variety—the very best in publishing today.

For complete information about books available from Penguin—including Puffins, Penguin Classics, and Arkana—and how to order them, write to us at the appropriate address below. Please note that for copyright reasons the selection of books varies from country to country.

In the United Kingdom: Please write to *Dept. JC, Penguin Books Ltd, FREEPOST, West Drayton, Middlesex UB7 0BR.*

If you have any difficulty in obtaining a title, please send your order with the correct money, plus ten percent for postage and packaging, to *P.O. Box No. 11, West Drayton, Middlesex UB7 0BR*

In the United States: Please write to *Consumer Sales, Penguin USA, P.O. Box 999, Dept. 17109, Bergenfield, New Jersey 07621-0120.* VISA and MasterCard holders call 1-800-253-6476 to order all Penguin titles

In Canada: Please write to *Penguin Books Canada Ltd, 10 Alcorn Avenue, Suite 300, Toronto, Ontario M4V 3B2*

In Australia: Please write to *Penguin Books Australia Ltd, P.O. Box 257, Ringwood, Victoria 3134*

In New Zealand: Please write to *Penguin Books (NZ) Ltd, Private Bag 102902, North Shore Mail Centre, Auckland 10*

In India: Please write to *Penguin Books India Pvt Ltd, 706 Eros Apartments, 56 Nehru Place, New Delhi 110 019*

In the Netherlands: Please write to *Penguin Books Netherlands bv, Postbus 3507, NL-1001 AH Amsterdam*

In Germany: Please write to *Penguin Books Deutschland GmbH, Metzlerstrasse 26, 60594 Frankfurt am Main*

In Spain: Please write to *Penguin Books S. A., Bravo Murillo 19, 1° B, 28015 Madrid*

In Italy: Please write to *Penguin Italia s.r.l., Via Felice Casati 20, I-20124 Milano*

In France: Please write to *Penguin France S. A., 17 rue Lejeune, F–31000 Toulouse*

In Japan: Please write to *Penguin Books Japan, Ishikiribashi Building, 2–5–4, Suido, Bunkyo-ku, Tokyo 112*

In Greece: Please write to *Penguin Hellas Ltd, Dimocritou 3, GR–106 71 Athens*

In South Africa: Please write to *Longman Penguin Southern Africa (Pty) Ltd, Private Bag X08, Bertsham 2013*